BLESSED ARE
THOSE WHO
Mourn

BLESSED ARE THOSE WHO
Mourn
Comforting Catholics in Their Time of Grief

GLENN M. SPENCER, JR.

Our Sunday Visitor Publishing Division
Our Sunday Visitor, Inc.
Huntington, Indiana 46750

Copyright © 1999 by Our Sunday Visitor Publishing Division, Our Sunday Visitor, Inc.

ISBN: 0-87973-946-0
LCCCN: 98-67326

Cover design by Monica Watts
PRINTED IN THE UNITED STATES OF AMERICA

946

Contents

Acknowledgments

There is a challenge in writing about how the Church understands, lives through, and even grows with the everyday crises of life. Today, most of these crises are like pieces of territory staked out and claimed by the psychological community, which takes its direction from science and philosophy. Our challenge as Catholics is learning how to retrieve some of this property as the Church's own, while remaining true to her God-given identity as the Body of Christ.

For many years I have had both feet planted firmly in the Church and in the psychological community, which has made this challenge ever-present for me.

Writing about grief is a good way to face that challenge. In the present case this task was less daunting for me because I have worked with two excellent editors from Our Sunday Visitor: Jim Manney and Henry O'Brien — two professionals who love both the Word and the word.

I also owe special thanks to Father Louis Tarsitano and Father Larry Wells for suggestions that improved this work greatly. Moreover, I appreciate the sustaining help and encouragement provided by Ann, Hannah, and the parish of All Saints. Finally, I wish to dedicate this book to my parents, Glenn and Margaret, who taught me the importance of books and people.

Introduction

The Sacramental Promise of the Broken Heart

The Spirit of the Lord GOD is upon me,
because the LORD has anointed me
to bring good tidings to the afflicted;
he has sent me to bind up the
brokenhearted, . . .
to give them a garland instead of ashes,
the oil of gladness instead of mourning,
the mantle of praise instead of a faint spirit;
that they may be called oaks of righteousness, . . .
— *ISAIAH 61:1-3*

Jesus preached his first sermon in his hometown synagogue just after his temptation in the wilderness. The focus of his sermon was the text from Isaiah, which proclaimed his mission of healing, particularly healing for the brokenhearted. Some months after that, as he and his disciples traveled to the grassy hills beyond the Jordan River, he delivered another sermon we call the Sermon on the Mount. He taught his disciples the secrets of the kingdom of God. And in that sermon, he once again drew attention to those who are living with grief: "Blessed are those who mourn, for they shall be comforted" (Matthew 5:4).

Much of Jesus' mission was to bind up the brokenhearted. He passed on his ministry of healing to the Apostles, and thus he passed it on to the Church. Our Lord's promise is that he will heal our broken hearts, comfort us, and lead us into a deeper experience of himself, of others, and of ourselves.

There have been many books written on the subject of grief and loss, especially since Dr. Elisabeth Kübler-

Ross's best seller *On Death and Dying*. There have been some excellent handbooks provided to us by pastoral-care theologians and physicians, like *Good Grief* by Granger E. Westberg. In recent years, with the explosion of the Christian counseling movement in the Protestant churches, many authors have offered helpful thoughts for those who mourn and guidance for the pastor who deals with grief in his own parish. But too often those books have taken a highly individualistic, psychological, and cognitive approach to Christian living. What is usually left out are the Church and the sacraments.

I would like to suggest another approach to the healing of grief. The one that is offered in this book is sacramental. It is not offered to the exclusion of the psychological and cognitive approach, but rather in addition to it. It is a "both-and" approach rather than an "either-or" one. It is rooted in our common life in the Catholic Church. The Catholic religion is a group thing. But it is not simply a voluntary association of like-minded people who gather for a common cause. We have been baptized into the Body of Christ, and thus we are not merely isolated individuals who have a relationship with God. We are members (as in hands, feet, eyes, and ears) of the Body of Christ, which is an organism, not merely an organization. And our relationship with God is initiated, sustained, and nourished through and in that life-giving organism. As Catholics, we approach grief from a sacramental point of view within the community that Christ gave birth to, namely his Church. Plainly put, from this point of view, grief may become a means of grace.

Our Common Life

Grief is essentially sacramental when it is experienced within the living community of the Body of Christ. It is through our common life in the Body that we come to experience the grace that God offers to us in our losses;

and thus we can make progress along the spiritual path already traveled by so many Christian saints through the centuries. Grief can lead to a new life of creativity and fullness. Bereavement can also lead to a new life of practical holiness. Catholic Christians are called, as Peter put it, to "become partakers of the divine nature." Jesus taught us in word and deed that the essence of the divine nature is self-giving love. Grief can become a means of participating in and growth in the self-giving love manifested in the life of our Lord. The *Catechism of the Catholic Church* makes the point that our suffering can be offered up to our Lord so that we can draw nearer to Christ in his passion: "By the grace of this sacrament the sick person receives the strength and the gift of uniting himself more closely to Christ's Passion: in a certain way he is *consecrated* to bear fruit by configuration to the Savior's redemptive Passion. Suffering, a consequence of original sin, acquires a new meaning; it becomes a participation in the saving work of Jesus" (No. 1521).

I want to suggest that through our common experience of bereavement we have the opportunity to consecrate it and offer it up to our Lord in such a way that it "acquires a new meaning." Grief provides the experience that can move a person to cultivate a disciplined prayer life and spiritual exercises that bring the soul closer to God. Bereavement is not merely a psychological state. It is that, but much more; from the Church's point of view bereavement is an opportunity for cooperation with the Holy Spirit. Bereavement may become a means of grace. "The way of the Cross" is both the experience of the broken heart and the sacramental way.

"Let It Be unto Me According to Thy Word"

Our Lady was told by old Simeon on the day of our Lord's circumcision: "This child is destined to be a sign which men will reject; he is set for the fall and the rising of many in Israel; and your own soul a sword shall pierce" (cf. Luke 2:34). The Church commemorates both the prophecy and her experience on the Feast of Our Lady of Sorrows. The opening prayer for that Mass, as found in the *Daily Roman Missal*, reads:

> Father,
> as your Son was raised on the cross,
> his mother Mary stood by him, sharing his
>   sufferings.
> May your Church be united with Christ
> in his suffering and death
> and so come to share in his rising to new life,
> where he lives and reigns with you and the Holy
>   Spirit,
> one God, for ever and ever.

All of our sorrows can be offered up to our Lord and thus in a sense we can share in his suffering. Mary is our perfect example. Her offering of herself — body and soul — included the cross of her Son. How many Christians have fed spiritually upon Michelangelo's *Pietà*, encouraged and uplifted by the fact that the Blessed Virgin knows by firsthand experience what sorrow feels like? Nowhere is God's grace more beautifully displayed than in the relationship between Jesus and Mary. The Church proclaims that Jesus is "the man of sorrows, acquainted with grief" (Isaiah 53:3). No one understands our broken hearts better than Jesus. The Church declares that it is he who "has borne our griefs / and carried our sorrows" (Isaiah 53:4). And Mary is the perfect model of the Church's reception of grace and submission to the will of God: "May it be done to me according to your word" (Luke 1:38, NAB).

What the Church has to offer is nothing new; indeed, it is ancient, and yet it may be new in its application for some people. How many broken hearts have been healed by self-examination, the sacrament of penance, and the reception of the Blessed Sacrament? How many people have known the joy and blessing of offering up the Eucharist as a special intention for a loved one or friend who is suffering or who has died? How many Catholics have grown in their spiritual lives by practicing the corporal and spiritual works of mercy in a conscious and intentional way? Grief and loss are a portal through which we may view eternity. The broken heart is a window through which our Lord offers us his own sacramental presence. Bereavement is a doorway through which we may ascend to a higher understanding and imitation of his own self-sacrificing love. An old European ballad speaks of God breaking his own heart in order to save mankind. It is the way God himself offers his love to us.

My Professional Experience in Grief and Pastoral Care

I have served as the pastor of five parishes, during which time I have participated in the most intimate and vulnerable experiences in the lives of my parishioners. In sickness and in health we have worked together in all these parishes to fulfill Jesus' new commandment to love one another. I have been in the emergency room after automobile accidents to be with the victims' loved ones; I have counseled couples in their marriages, lonely singles, confused adolescents; I have tried to be there for those involved in post-abortion grief and guilt, suicides, and the normal experience of death. I have done premarital counseling and what is now referred to as pre-premarital counseling!

I have also served as the director of pastoral care in a psychiatric hospital where I spent hundreds of hours with all ages of people in deep distress and grief. I worked with people who were clinically depressed and anxious as well as those who were suffering from chemical dependency.

After I finished my seminary studies at Duke Divinity School, I entered the Clinical Pastoral Education program at Duke Medical Center. That was an intense, challenging, and very rewarding experience for me. And that is where I first realized just how wide the grief experience is, through the patients assigned to me, through theological reflection, and, just as importantly, through personal experience. My supervisor, Logan Jones, a Moravian minister, was especially effective in helping me see how grief and loss are a part of our whole life and they include more than death and dying.

This book is a result of my ministry among the people of God in those parishes and in the psychiatric hospital. The case examples that are used throughout this book are true. But a psychiatric chaplain, and especially a priest, has to be chiefly sensitive to confidentiality. For that reason identity, time, and place are altered to protect confidentiality. Needless to say, I make no reference whatsoever in these pages to any sacramental confession. I have been with these people as their pastor during the most important turning points in their lives. I can think of no greater honor in the world than being invited by them to be their pastor. And thus the accounts herein are intended to honor them by providing instruction and encouragement for others.

Who Should Read This Book?

This work is written with a commitment to help people understand the grieving process from within the Church. That is not to say that only Catholics would be able to benefit from its pages. I hope that any serious Christian who is experiencing grief or who has a friend or relative who is going through grief and loss would grow from the thoughts and ideas contained here. This is a book that a parish priest or social worker or hospice counselor could give to a parishioner or client who is grieving a loss in order to educate, console, inspire, and challenge him or her. It is also a book that a parish priest or hospice center might use to conduct a class on grief and loss or to help the members establish a support group. In short, *Blessed Are Those Who Mourn* is the kind of book that any Catholic Christian could benefit from reading. He or she will learn not only how to grow from our grief experience, but also how to be better friends to those who are grieving.

When you have finished *Blessed Are Those Who Mourn*, you will better understand:

❀ That grief and loss include more than the deaths of loved ones.

❀ That the experience of grief and loss is universal.

❀ That there is an order to the experience of grief and loss.

❀ That the Church herself has experienced the process of grief and loss.

❀ How denial works.

❀ How to cope with special problems like holiday grief.

❀ The potential for medical complications and grief.

❀ Complicated grief and the grief of children.

❀ The special strength of Catholics.

❀ What part forgiveness plays in our healing.

❀ What to do about our feelings.

❀ How to find others who have experienced loss.

❀ How to form a grief-and-loss group in your parish.

❀ What part the sacraments play in your healing.

❀ How to handle anger.

Self-giving Love

As Jesus traveled the dusty roads of Palestine with his little flock of disciples, he greeted, blessed, and healed the brokenhearted. He confronted death and triumphed over it. He lived a perfect life of self-giving love.

The great spiritual directors all tell us that self-giving love is the *telos* of our being — our purpose for existing. We have all experienced broken hearts, broken dreams, broken relationships, and broken spirits. We are just like the people in the Gospels — needy. Because of that, we can expect the same response from our Lord. Just as his presence healed people and made them whole then, so his sacramental presence heals us and makes us whole today. Our bereavement can be the doorway to our healing, an ascent to a life that resembles his life — a life of creativity and fullness, and of self-giving love.

1 Grief Is Everywhere

Grief is the natural human response to a significant loss. Grief is a predictable and well-charted human experience that transcends gender, nationality, culture, religion, and time. Grief is universal and it includes all kinds of losses, not only the loss of a loved one through death.

Grief is not always easy to explain or define with precision. But we all instinctively know grief when we hear it.

We heard grief in the voices of Korean mothers and fathers as they stood at the foot of a mountain in Guam calling the names of their daughters after a passenger jet full of vacationers crashed into the mountainside.

In the Bible we hear it poignantly in the voice of Mary Magdalene on the morning of the Resurrection. In the garden she stooped to look into the tomb and found it empty. Two angels sat where the body of Jesus had been laid. "Why are you weeping?" they asked Mary. "They have taken my Lord away," she replied, "and I don't know where they have put him" (cf. John 20:11-13).

We know grief when we see it.

Walking through the mall we see a woman sitting by a fountain, weeping quietly.

A man discusses his crumbling career with a trusted friend. He looks crushed, beaten down by months of grief and worry.

A couple struggle to hold their life together in a counselor's office; the grief is written all over their faces.

Grief is tangible and substantive. It attaches itself to all of our losses in degrees. But grief isn't as chaotic as it seems at first. It has a pattern. And knowledge of that pattern provides us with a set of tools that helps us effectively and maturely move through the normal everyday ups and downs and even the tragedies of life.

People involved in pastoral care have discovered that when we are trying to make sense of an experience of violence, or death, or betrayal, or of any loss, there is a common set of experiences that we can count on and a common set of tasks that helps us work through them. And I am suggesting that these patterns transcend particular cultural expressions of grief and encompass a vast range of our experiences of loss. Grief is the way of all flesh.

Before we look at the common patterns, let us consider some of the many ways that grief touches our lives.

The Death of a Loved One

We limit our understanding of bereavement if we were to think only in terms of the death of loved ones. However, that is the place to begin, since in losing friends and family to death, grief becomes intensely focused.

A few years ago one of my best friends, Lou, died suddenly. A robust young priest, seemingly in the prime of his life, Lou died from the complications of an aneurysm. A squadron of doctors and nurses tried to save him while I stood there simply dumbfounded. Several of the emergency room staff wept as I administered last rites to him. I have never felt so helpless in my life. Except for the sacrament, there was nothing I could do. Even as I spoke the words of absolution, it was as though I were listening to someone else talk.

A priest-friend of mine recalls the morning his grandmother died. He was about nine years old and he had never experienced the death of anyone very close to him. His grandmother had been rushed that night to the hospital in the small southern town where she lived. He recalled all the confusion in the home. The hurried banging on the door. The fear in the faces of his father and mother. The whirling light of the ambulance.

The next morning his mother came home looking exhausted. She asked him to ride with her to the hospital. The priest said he could still recall the very curve he and his mother were rounding thirty-six years before when she told him that his grandmother had died. "I literally felt as though someone had socked me in the chest and knocked the breath out of me. The first word out of my mouth was 'No!' My grandmother and I were very close. I became depressed after her death, but I didn't know it. Now I know it."

Another priest recalls the death of his grandmother — his "St. Monica" — when he was a little child. His grandmother was one of the most important women in his life in his early years. She taught him to pray, to believe in God, to see a bigger and brighter world than the natural one right before his eyes.

"I remember once," he said, "coming upon her accidentally in her bedroom and finding her upon her knees praying privately. I still recall the feeling of awe, and the sense of the presence of God in her life. I felt I was on holy ground.

"The night she died my parents had rushed her to the hospital. My mother told me of her death the next morning. I was stunned. It was simply unthinkable that she was not going to be with me any longer. Over the next year I felt all the grief: sadness, depression, denial, anger. It was years before I learned that I could offer my grief up to the Lord."

One ordinary Wednesday several years ago Bobby and Jean took their three-year-old daughter, Becky, to the doctor because the little girl kept falling down. The family doctor sent them to the university hospital the next day. By Friday afternoon the surgeons had scheduled Becky for surgery. A tumor was growing in her brain.

"I can't believe this is happening," Bobby said over and over again as he and his wife spent time with the chaplain in the hospital. They prayed for a miracle. Becky became their whole focus. By the end of the first month they had gone through a crash course in oncology and grief.

There's a pattern here: shock, unbelief, feelings of unreality and helplessness followed by sadness and depression. Whether it is in the hospital, the pastor's study, the nursing home, or the family room, we have gone through a common experience — a common pattern of grief and loss. We have all traveled the same path, even though each one has experienced the landmarks and crossroads uniquely. Like people hiking a trail in the mountains or walking a path by the sea, we have a common road and a common goal we travel when it comes to grief.

Losing What We Have

Getting Old

We in the boomer generation see our lives changing. What has been familiar and satisfying is becoming strange and troubling.

I work out at a gym four or five days a week. I started regular exercise in my forties, and what really surprised me was how many other boomers are doing the same thing in an effort to stay healthy, to look healthy, and to keep up with our kids. Yet — we are growing old. Youth is brief. Comedians of our generation are fashioning their routines around the subject of aging. We laugh at them as they make fun of their thinning hair and wrinkles, their waning libido, and their low energy level. Recently, *Time* magazine printed an article on the hormone DHE, which promises a testosterone surge and an anti-aging formula for men of our graying generation. Within two weeks nutrition centers in several major cities sold out of the drug.

But as every generation has learned since Juan Ponce de León thought he had discovered the fountain of youth in Florida, youth is fleeting. So we learn how to laugh at our condition, and we begin to take aging seriously, something we have avoided throughout our lives. For some, this is a constructive realization. We begin to recognize the opportunity to use the gifts and graces we have acquired over the years for the benefit of others. Recently I heard from a friend my age who is opting for early retirement from a successful career in the communications industry. She is returning to college to study social work so she can make her contribution in a new way that will give a deeper meaning to her life.

Kissing Mom and Dad Good-bye

Many boomers have had a difficult time simply growing up and separating from Mom and Dad in a healthy and productive way. Albert Brooks's movie *Mother* deals humorously with this issue. In this movie, Albert Brooks plays the part of a middle-aged man who has come to the conclusion that somehow his mother is to blame for all his misery in relationships. He hits upon the idea of moving back home with his widowed mom and taking up residence in his old room. He intends to discover the mother-induced flaw in his relationship with women. What he ends up discovering is that his mom wasn't nearly as attached to him as he was to her. He was in many ways still a big baby.

Many of us know exactly what St. Paul meant about growing up — "When I was a child, I spoke like a child, I thought like a child, I reasoned like a child; when I became a man, I gave up childish ways" (1 Corinthians 13:11) — except when it comes to our parents. Around our parents, it's difficult not to become childish again. We have to grow up in terms of our relationship with our parents. But at some point we have to "kiss Mom and Dad good-bye" in the emotional and spiritual sense. All of this becomes more difficult when we see our parents experiencing chronic ill health, depression, and sometimes isolation.

A close friend told me that one of his earliest memories as a child is sitting on his father's shoulders so he could see the cowboys riding their horses in the Thanksgiving parade in his hometown.

"My father was a strong man," he said, "but now he walks with steps that are unsure and rickety. He had major surgery for cancer a few years ago, and his convalescence has been both physically and emotionally painful for him. My mother has had a major heart attack. They still take care of each other, but the day may come when that will not be possible. The cheery-faced young man that once hoisted me upon his shoulders to see the cowboys now needs support to walk."

The tables are being turned on our generation, and it is time for us to step forward and take on parentlike responsibilities for our parents. That is difficult for a generation that has been as self-centered as ours. But it is another opportunity to grow into the self-giving love that we have received from our heavenly Father.

Moving On

There was a time, not really that long ago, when we could count on staying in the same community our whole lives. We were a rooted people. Generations had belonged to the same parish, lived on the same street, graduated from the same school. Towns and communities were small, secrets were hard to keep, and families were well-known in the community for generations. Our lives were predictable and ordered.

That is simply no longer the case. It is hard to imagine a culture more transient than ours now. American families can assume that they will move on average seven or eight times before retirement. What is astonishing is that it isn't astonishing anymore. We take it for granted that our presence in any given community is only transitory. I once knew a priest who was raised by a single mother who moved no less than twenty times before he was nineteen years old! That's an extreme case, but moving is the norm. Priests such as myself get used to parishes full of families that move on after two or three years. Dad or Mom gets a promotion or a better job offer. They finish graduate school. New and brighter opportunities loom on the horizon and lure us into the future.

We say we're used to moving on, yet when we do, we suffer loss. Frequently, devastating loss.

Maggie was in tears for weeks after she and Bob and their four children moved from Connecticut to Atlanta. She had been happy there, very happy indeed. Bob was a fashion designer with a national company. He was highly prized by the CEO. His designs and ideas had made a lot of money for the company, and he was proud of his work. They were all happy. They had good schools, good neighbors, and a great parish. And then came the opportunity — an offer from a respected competitor to take over a division. Maggie and Bob talked it over and prayed over it. They discussed it with their priest and asked for his prayers and then they decided to make the move.

The first few weeks were a whirlwind of activity, but underneath it all was a sort of sad undertow pulling at Maggie's heart. She was teary most of the time. She liked their house in Atlanta and she had found a good school for the kids. But her heart ached for Connecticut.

She missed her friends and especially her parish where she had been involved with her children's catechesis program. But she worked to put all this out of her mind. She was being stoic about it. Nine months passed in their new home before Maggie admitted that she was depressed — really depressed. "It's as though someone had died," she told her best friend in Connecticut over the phone. "I've planted flowers; I've wallpapered; I've gotten involved in a women's Bible study; but there is this deep sadness I can't shake." Transplanting a plant, a tree, or a flower is traumatic. Special care has to be given to increase the chances of successful rooting. Uprooting for an individual or a family is traumatic as well. We need to realize that even though our culture is increasingly transient, the experience is traumatizing.

The parish is a community in the lives of many Catholics. Unfortunately the transience of modern life instills a sense of independence rather than interdependence when it comes to parish commitment. A parish isn't a place to warehouse Christians. It is a local expression of the Church, and yet the potential for commitment, transformation, happiness, and service simply goes unfulfilled for many Christians because of the internalized sense of transience. And when geographical moves have to be made over and over again, they take a toll on the family and parish life.

Getting Downsized

Another loss that has a powerful impact upon the individual and the family and even whole communities is the loss of a job. A case in point is the story of Susan, a nurse administrator on the substance-abuse wing of a psychiatric hospital for eleven years.

All week long the administrators had worked behind closed doors in the hospital. They even taped paper over the windows so the staff couldn't see into the rooms where they met. It was obvious that some crisis had come upon the hospital. It had to do with the advent of HMOs — Health Maintenance Organizations. HMOs were changing the relationship between the patients and the hospital. The time allotted for the patient's stay in the hospital had been drastically cut from twenty-one days to seven or even three days. It was a bewildering experience for the doctors and staff as they sought to provide care to patients under radically constricted circumstances. The hospital administration had to learn to navigate new and choppy financial waters.

The next Monday morning, staff members found out how that was to be accomplished. The work force was cut by one fifth. Susan was fired. As she walked to her green Volkswagen beetle that morning with a cardboard box that held her personal items, she felt completely numb. She had not seen it coming at all. With her tenure, her experience, her knowledge of the recovering community, she thought her job was secure. It wasn't. Her position was eliminated, and those in administration had spread her responsibilities out to three other nurses. Now, at fifty-five, Susan was looking for a job.

But she had become so angry over her firing that she was sometimes afraid to apply for a job. She had thought of the hospital as a second family. Now she felt she had become only a means to an end for the hospital.

Her anger found its focus on one administrator in particular: Nina, whom Susan had considered a good friend and colleague. They had come to the hospital about the same time and had moved up in the ranks together. But Nina survived the job cuts. Susan's anger smoldered. Her job search was unsuccessful for months. Finally, more than a year after her firing, she had to settle for a job of lesser pay and lesser status.

Susan's experience of "downsizing" had colored her whole life. She felt stuck in her anger. She no longer felt joy in working with her patients. She was afraid she was becoming a hard and bitter person. Even with all of her training, it had not occurred to Susan that she was grieving the loss of her job. Her prestige, her peers, the family atmosphere on the wing, as well as the income and benefits — all of these things were gone. It was like a death to her. When she saw that, she realized that she had become mired in her anger and it was indeed turning into bitterness.

Betrayal

The Bible is full of stories of betrayal. In a sense, betrayal is at the very heart of what has gone wrong in God's creation. The devil, originally created by God as an angel of great beauty and knowledge, betrayed the Creator when he sought to lead a rebellion against God and supplant him (cf. Isaiah 14:12-20). One way to think about sin is to think of it in terms of betrayal. Adam and Eve betrayed God. Their children betrayed one another and then they betrayed God. Probably the most well-known case of treachery is Judas's betrayal of our Lord. We have it forever memorialized for us in the Eucharist: "On the night in which he was betrayed, he took bread . . ." (cf. Matthew 26:20-29, Mark 14:17-25, and Luke 22:14-23). Literally from Genesis to Revelation the Bible tells the story of human betrayal and its bitter fruit.

David, a man who betrayed many and was himself betrayed, sings of the bitterness of betrayal:

> All who hate me whisper together about me;
>> they imagine the worst for me.
> They say, "A deadly thing has fastened upon him;
>> he will not rise again from where he lies."
> Even my bosom friend in whom I trusted,
>> who ate of my bread, has lifted his heel
>>> against me.
>
> — PSALM 41:7-9

From this perspective, man's own redemption may be viewed as God's faithfulness in holding on to us in the face of our constant betrayals of him. The life of Jeremiah and his prophecy is a poignant example of how our betrayals break our friendship with God.

Sadly, the same story continues unabated. What is more painful than betrayal? Susan, the nurse who was "downsized" from her position in the hospital, experienced the pain all the more sharply because she understood it as the betrayal of a close friend. Whether it is in business or in the parish or between siblings or in a marriage, few things hurt as badly. Some would say that even death itself is not as difficult to accept as being betrayed by a friend or a loved one.

After the funeral of a young mother, the husband said to his priest: "I thank God that it was only her death. We loved each other and were faithful to one another. I feel like I'm going to die sometimes, but it's clean. We had no regrets of our own creation." The priest was taken aback. But in time he understood what the young father meant. His grief for his wife was focused upon her death and not mingled with other losses like unfaithfulness that could have occurred from their willfulness and sin.

Losing the Future

When Dreams Don't Come True

We boomers remember Woodstock. There was something back then people referred to as the "Woodstock Experience." I'm not sure what all that meant at the time, but at least a piece of it had to do with having big dreams. We thought we could change the world. There were few limits that we had come up against at that time. And there was a sort of defiance that went along with testing limits.

Now we know about limits — and disappointment. A comment I've heard often in counseling is, "I didn't think it was going to turn out this way." As we grow older, we boomers discover that the world has changed us rather than the other way around. All of this brings grief and loss in its wake.

A scene in the movie *Sleepless in Seattle* expresses much of the fantasy of our day when it comes to relationships. It's the one where Meg Ryan and Tom Hanks have finally met at the top of the Empire State Building. They are simply perfect. After near misses they have found true love. They embrace, with the lights of New York City twinkling below like stars fallen from heaven. This is a fairy tale. True love, we are told by our popular culture, looks like this.

But it's not — and as we age we learn the bitter truth about fantasies like this. In a society that raises the icon of *Sleepless in Seattle* to such heights, fifty-one percent of marriages end in divorce. Though relationships often start out with romantic fireworks, eventually, sooner rather than later, people have to get down to the day-in-and-day-out business of taking care of a marriage. We don't do a very good job of this. It's not easy to imagine Meg Ryan or Tom Hanks or Julia Roberts or George Clooney swabbing down the commode. Or getting two or three kids ready for church on Sunday morning. Or parenting a bewildered adolescent with genuine grace and love. But someone has to do it, and most of us can't afford an au pair or a governess.

Many of us in the Woodstock generation dreamed of community. A fairly common dream was that community would just *happen*. There is a scene in the movie *Metropolitan* where two twenty-something men are talking to an older man about their former expectations in life. At one point the older man makes a point about friendships that went something like this: "In college I used to look around at my friends and think, 'These people are going to be my friends for the rest of my life,' but it didn't work out that way. I hardly see any of them anymore."

It is a hard lesson to learn: Community doesn't just *happen*. It must be consciously and intentionally pursued and worked for. And once attained to any degree, community has to be taken care of like any living thing.

We uproot community in the pursuit of other dreams. But these dreams frequently are not realized either. Many people are finding that they simply have not experienced the financial success or the career success they expected in their youth. Too often both husband and wife have to work to make ends meet, since personal earning power is below expectations. Still they struggle.

And if it is not a matter of making enough money to raise a family, it is a matter of prestige and position. I once heard a woman say that she hated meeting the people she went to school with because they inevitably asked what she did for a living. "Oh, I make plenty of money," she said, "but my vocation doesn't matter." In her eyes she simply had not made it in life. More and more people are changing the way they live and think about this issue. I recently had a conversation with a man who turned down a promotion with his firm because it entailed a geographical move that would uproot his wife and children.

Infertility

When couples are young and newly married, they just assume that their family will grow and they will have children. When it doesn't happen, both husband and wife are tried to the limit. Jamie and Edward's story is a case in point.

Mother's Day was especially hard on Jamie. She and Edward had always assumed that when they were ready they would have children. But they had been married for eleven years and they still had not been blessed with children. Jamie had not even become pregnant. They wanted children. Jamie dreamed about babies and about being pregnant.

They went to a fertility specialist and started on a long road that led to a lot of disappointments. Jamie had started doubting the justice of God in all of this, especially when she saw babies that were not cared for and when she thought about the abortion industry. Once while shopping at the mall she even had an urge to snatch a toddler from a mother when she appeared to be unresponsive to the baby's crying. Jamie wondered if she was going crazy. At times she felt as though her emotions were in the driver's seat and she was the passenger. At times she felt as though her life were careening wildly out of her control.

About two years into the process with the fertility specialist, Jamie and Edward had a big argument. They had argued before, and their counselor had given them a set of rules on how to argue fairly. But this argument was different. It went on most of Saturday, and when they went to bed they both had a feeling that they had crossed some invisible line. After a few days they both realized that the invisible line they had crossed was the realization that they were not going to have children. That was a biting reality for them. They had lost their dream, their future, and they had to grieve the loss.

Abortion

The primary victim of abortion is the unborn child. But there are other victims too, and they grieve. The sadness of mothers who have had abortions illustrates the power of grief to insist upon attention.

I met Robbie, a forty-seven-year-old lawyer, in a grief-and-loss support group in a hospital. She was weepy most of the time and she shared little with her group that was threatening for her. One afternoon she asked to meet privately with a nurse she had become close to and with whom she had built some trust. She told the nurse the story of her abortion over twenty-five years earlier. Robbie had never been political about abortion, and had always felt sorry for the women involved. Single, she was in her first year of law school when she became pregnant. Her decision to abort the child was painful from the beginning. She knew it was wrong. After the abortion she went right back to school, although she had several periods of extended sadness and weeping. She managed to stifle it all and attend to her schoolwork.

Three years later she married and a year after that she had a child. A girl. At that time she went into a deep depression and saw a psychologist for a while. Now, years later, her own daughter was getting married and the old, unresolved issue rose to the foreground of her life. Robbie was raised a Catholic, but she had not been to church in years. After her session with the nurse, she asked to see a priest. She wanted to deal with her sense of guilt and shame and sadness spiritually. She longed to return to the Church. The whole occasion became a new beginning for Robbie. In the sacrament of reconciliation she found forgiveness and a new start.

Our generation came of age when abortion was legalized in this nation. Millions of women have been ravaged by grief over their abortions. In my work in the parish and a psychiatric hospital, I have seen the grief and the profound depression that often linger for years in mothers who have had abortions. I have also seen the healing and reconciliation that can occur in their lives and in the lives of their families through the sacrament of penance and the love of the people in the Church. Here, too, our Lord is prepared "to give to them a garland instead of ashes, / the oil of gladness instead of mourning" (Isaiah 61:3). The sacrament of reconciliation is a wonderful miracle-working sacrament.

Another loss often overlooked in our day is the death of the unborn by miscarriage. In my pastoral experience, it often takes three or four years for a woman to assimilate the death of a child in this manner. So many things don't happen that happen with other deaths. People don't usually gather for a wake. The mother and father don't receive messages of condolences from friends and family. Often the priest isn't even informed of the death, and if he is, he may not know exactly how to respond himself. But the unborn was a child. Just ask any mother who has experienced a miscarriage. The baby is real. And the grief is real.

Victims of Violence

Our nation watched in complete unbelief and disgust a video showing a group of L.A. policemen beating Rodney King with nightsticks and shocking him with Taser guns. The men were tried and released. Once again television brought the horror of violence into our living rooms as we watched the riots after the trial. One of the most unforgettable images from the L.A. riots is the beating of Reginald Denny as he was dragged from his truck by rampaging rioters. Denny was pelted, kicked, and stoned. He was left for dead. And he almost did die. He went through months of painful rehabilitation. The event changed Denny's life in many ways. Most importantly, it became for him an opportunity for a spiritual awakening. He seemed intent upon making a Christian end to the matter, and it was arranged for him to meet with the men who had participated in his beating. William Willimon and Stanley Hauerwas in their book on the Lord's Prayer refer to this event and make an interesting observation: "After his painful recovery, (Mr. Denny) met face to face with his attackers, shook hands with them and forgave them. A reporter, commenting on the scene, wrote, 'It is said that Mr. Denny is suffering from brain damage.'"

The reporter probably speaks for most of us. To some degree anyway our first reaction is unbelief when we observe grace in action. But Mr. Denny didn't start out with a forgiving heart toward these men who did him real and permanent harm. The months of recovery were not merely physical recovery, but they entailed emotional and spiritual recovery as well. Forgiveness of this sort is an achievement. It takes work — not, of course, work done apart from the Holy Spirit. It isn't an achievement that we can accomplish apart from the prompting and assistance of the Holy Spirit. But forgiveness is an act of self-sacrificing love that simply doesn't come naturally to us. And so it strikes us as remarkable that anyone could forgive such an unjust act as the beating of Mr. Denny. And most of us find it especially difficult to move beyond our own anger and the desire for revenge against the person who has violated us.

Violence has become more and more common in our nation. Maybe it has always been this way, but certainly a spotlight has been thrown on it in the last few years. There is hardly a family untouched by violence in some form. And often the violence is generated within the family itself. Catholics believe in the family. God instituted marriage for the very purpose of growing and nurturing families. But even Christian marriages and Christian families are composed of sinful men and women. Not only do we sin against one another, but we too are sinned against. A family can be a cocoon of safety and nurturance or it can be a place of violence. If the practice of forgiveness isn't nurtured and taught in the family, we will raise a generation of disabled Catholics. Later in this book we will look at family systems in order to see how they may help or hinder the members of the family work through the grief that we must process in the course of our lives.

Terminal Illness

Elisabeth Kübler-Ross's first book, *On Death and Dying*, was largely an account of how people grieve through a terminal illness. Her focus was not only upon the person with the terminal illness but also on the person's family and friends as well. It is instructive how our views of terminal illness have changed over the centuries.

People in our day and time fear terminal illness above all else. Someone observed that if they had the choice, Americans would prefer to die in their sleep without knowing it. But such has not always been the case. In the Middle Ages and at other times in history, terminal illness was viewed as the preferred manner of death because it gave the person the opportunity to set his affairs in order and to settle any unfinished business between friends or family. A sudden, unexpected death was feared because those very opportunities were left unfinished and the person potentially was not in a state of grace. Many of the older litanies, especially penitential ones, contain prayers for protection from sudden, unexpected death. Still, in our day the first reaction to the news of a terminal illness is often paralyzing fear. Only after some time of bargaining with God does the person begin to use the opportunity to his spiritual benefit.

Jack had been a history professor in a major university most of his adult life. He and his wife, Mary, raised four children, all of whom were married and well into making their way through life with their own families. Retirement had not been in the picture for Jack. Then during a routine visit to the family doctor he discovered that he had colon cancer. The cancer had progressed so far that surgery was required immediately.

Jack called his priest and filled him in and asked if he could stop by the hospital and visit with the family before the surgery and say a prayer. His faith in God was a guiding principle in his life. In his teaching, research, and in his family life Jack always assumed the truthfulness and virtue of the Catholic faith. He was not turning back at this point. Jack passed this legacy on to each of his children. When his priest arrived to visit the family the evening before the operation, the whole family had gathered in Jack's hospital room. There were all teary-eyed, but they were making a heroic effort to be positive. Mary was very protective of Jack. And Jack in return was busy boosting the faith of his children and consoling them. His priest anointed him and prayed for his healing. The next morning their priest arrived in time for them to have prayer together in Jack's room just before the operation.

The surgery was successful. Jack began chemotherapy after that and lived for another two years. He retired from teaching and spent the rest of his time with Mary and the children. His priest said that he felt a real sense of honor to have spent some of that time with Jack, Mary, and their family. Those two years were a roller-coaster ride for the whole family, especially Jack and

Mary. Hope bloomed brightly several times, only to be dimmed by recurring cancer. But the time was not wasted. Jack loved his family. He loved his vocation and his students. He loved Mary, whom he called his "sweetheart." And he loved God. Jack grieved like a Christian; he experienced real grief, shattering grief at times, but never hopeless grief.

Grief in Our Culture

Ours is a culture in the throes of major transitions. Grief puts a magnifying glass upon the conflicts that naturally rise from those transitions. At the same time, it highlights the depth of grief's possibilities for healing, its richness as a spiritual experience.

A Nation in Mourning

A few years ago I was at the University of Virginia Medical Center for an MRI. I had torn my rotator cuff, and the surgeon ordered several routine tests before the surgery. The experience of going through a battery of tests — X rays, blood test, urinalysis, and the MRI — was a test in itself. I finally finished the process after about five hours, and as I was leaving the hospital I noticed that in each waiting room I passed, the people were huddled around the television. Something had happened. I ducked into one of the rooms and watched as a news reporter stood at considerable distance from what remained of the Alfred P. Murrah Federal Building in Oklahoma City. Helicopters circled overhead with cameramen giving us a bird's-eye view of the wreckage. The front of the building had been blown away by an apparent terrorist attack. We all stood or sat there in stunned silence as the reporters tried to give us updated information on the tragedy.

We soon knew the grim facts: 168 people had been killed. Scores were still missing. A forty-eight-hundred-pound fertilizer bomb had been detonated in front of the building. The blast had ripped through the heart of the city and its people. Unbelievably, a nursery full of children had been on the front row just above the blast. Only a few of the children survived.

Over the next few days the pastors of the city counseled the grieving. As they listened to thousands of people, parishioners and nonparishioners alike, they tried to help them make sense of this tragedy. And they tried to make sense of it for themselves as well. People were filled with anger, sadness, and guilt.

Some weeks later when Billy Graham spoke to a congregation of thousands from the city, he made some astonishing comments. "We are here with you to let the healing begin," he said. "We are here to show you that a nation stands beside you in your grief. We are here to forgive."

Remarkable words. Some would even say, unnatural words, especially the part about forgiving. This is the sort of thing we say we believe, but how well do we practice it? And how can we understand and live with this peculiarly Christian answer in the light of raging emotions like anger, sadness, and guilt? Emotions that seem to be at odds with our best self. Emotions that seem to threaten the very foundations of what we believe. Is there a limit to healing for Christians? Is there a limit to forgiveness? Is it possible to go too far with this? Indeed, we all have the image forever in our minds of the firefighter cradling the lifeless baby in his arms standing outside the rubble of the federal office building in Oklahoma City. Does talk about forgiveness in this context seem to mock the amazing devastation of that image?

Three Deaths

It was August 31, 1997 — Sunday morning — before most of us heard that Diana Spencer, the Princess of Wales, had been killed in an automobile accident in Paris. We were all stunned and saddened by the death of the beautiful young princess who had already endured so many heartaches. We knew too much about her most personal and private suffering throughout the years since her marriage to Charles. Then we saw the picture of her armor-plated automobile smashed like a tin toy. The next week her death and funeral dominated the news. Many people in America sat up into the wee hours of the morning to watch Diana's funeral procession as it was broadcast live from England.

Not only England but much of the world entered a collective grief experience. The people of England were enraged that the royal family apparently did not share in their grief for the "people's princess." The feelings were so strong and the drumbeat so constant that Queen Elizabeth tried to answer the doubts and feelings of the people with a public and rather personal statement about Diana. And Diana's brother, in his funeral address, took the opportunity to vent — albeit in somewhat coded form — his anger toward the royal family and the press.

How should we grieve? Many people in England were angered by what appeared to be a cold and unfeeling response from the royal family. These were two different worlds on a collision course. Even weeks later when Prince Charles spoke of the death of Diana in moving terms, his insistence upon the importance of mourning with "dignity" was lost on many. Here were major cultural differences even within the same country. The same is true in our own nation, and these cultural transitions have brought on confusion and uprooting.

During that same week Mother Teresa died. Again the world, it seems, was thrust into a collective experience of grief. And yet it was markedly different from the grief experience we had concerning Diana. Our grief over Mother Teresa's death was not so full of anger and guilt.

The deep, profound sadness was certainly there upon the face of the Indian people who had lost such a friend. But the anger and guilt that seemed to be in the foreground during the initial period of grief for Diana were absent in Mother Teresa's case. Why the difference?

Viktor Frankl, a psychologist and survivor of the Holocaust, died as well that same week. Frankl wrote *Man's Search for Meaning*, a book that many of us read in high school or college. Frankl was a psychologist who was imprisoned in Auschwitz during World War II. Frankl survived while most of his friends died. He endured. But not only did he endure, he came out of the concentration camp with a clarified vision of life. And that vision he distilled into his book that was a sort of gift to the world.

Frankl, a Jew, experienced a profound Christian truth. There came a turning point for him in that living hell where he was stripped and tortured over and over again. Everything was taken from him by the Nazis. But in the midst of incredible suffering he discovered his freedom. He discovered something that no one could take from him by privation or torture or fear. Frankl said that he discovered, as he was being tortured by the guards, the transforming power of love. His captors could not determine the attitude that he would hold toward them. There was his true freedom. There was his only freedom. His will to love. Remarkable. Frankl's experience of violence and his discovery of the transforming power of love have helped many a Christian not only survive but grow through sorrowful experiences.

Grief casts a wide net in our lives. Though we usually think first of the death of a loved one when we think of bereavement, we can see from the stories we have looked at that grief enters into our lives from many directions. We will now turn our attention to the structures of that common experience.

2 Grief: "Catholic" and Catholic

Grief is an experience common to all humanity. It transcends culture and time. It is "catholic" — that is, "universal."

Grief is also Catholic. It is a well-charted experience in the Scriptures, in the lives of the saints, as well as in our common life in the Body of Christ. The same experience of grief that the Old Testament patriarchs and the New Testament disciples experienced is recognized in the lives of everyday Christians struggling to be faithful to God and to lead happy lives. In the living context of hard losses and biting reality, Catholics learn to face the chances and changes of life with grace and wisdom.

Our task is to live this universal, or catholic, pattern of grief as Catholics. And the interplay between these two dimensions of grief — catholic and Catholic — contains much of the power and mystery of God's plan for how we human beings deal with loss.

The Universal Pattern of Grief

Over the last thirty years or so, psychologists and pastoral counselors have come to understand the psychosocial stages of grief. Though there may be variations on how our grief is expressed from culture to culture, the multilayered experience of grief has a discernible form, pattern, and process. The universality and predictability of the stages or layers of grief allow the priest, the social worker, psychologist, friend, or family member to help the grieving person through his or her experience. An appreciation of the order of grief also allows the caregiver to attend faithfully to his or her own grief. It hardly makes sense to attempt to help others if we ourselves have fallen like blind men into the pit of ignorance.

Convergence — The Pattern of Bereavement

"Convergence" is what scientists call the tendency of human beings to follow a few basic patterns of behavior that transcend time and culture. Grief falls into one of these patterns. Robert M. Sapolsky, a biologist, wrote in *The Sciences* magazine (November-December 1994 issue) about his personal encounter with grief as the result of dealing with the death of his father. He was overwhelmed by emotions, even though his father's death followed a long illness and was much anticipated. A medical student in his laboratory reminded Sapolsky of the stages of grief first popularized by Dr. Elisabeth Kübler-Ross in her book *On Death and Dying*. Kübler-Ross saw terminally ill patients and their families going through stages of denial, anger, bargaining, depression, and acceptance.

Sapolsky thought that he himself had experienced these stages. He took great solace in the knowledge that his suffering was not unique but was universal. Somehow if we experience a pattern that is common to us all, we have a symbol of our oneness, an unmistakable family resemblance. Sapolsky sums up his thoughts this way: "Look at the image of a survivor of some carnage and, knowing nothing of her language, culture, beliefs or circumstances, you can still recognize in the fixed action patterns of her facial muscles the unmistakable lineaments of grief. That instant recognition, the universal predictability of certain aspects of human beings, whether in a facial expression or in the stages of mourning, is an emblem of our kinship and an imperative of empathy."

Sapolsky's "emblem of our kinship" is comforting. It is an attempt to find a spiritual answer to the hard realities of death and loss.

The "emblem of our kinship" for Catholics is found in nature and grace. First, in nature, in our creation, we are formed "in the image of God." As we are told in Genesis: "God created man in the image of himself, in the image of God he created him, male and female he created them" (1:27).

Thus from a Christian point of view we all have our common origin in God the Father. He is our Father, the Father of all mankind, through creation — a fundamental basis for our kinship as human beings.

But for Catholics the bond of kinship is deeper still. The bond established through the sacrament of baptism in the name of the Trinity makes us children of God in a supernatural sense. Through the sacrament of the new birth we are made children of God by adoption and grace. This is the new creation that finds its source in the new Adam, Jesus Christ, and in the response of the new Eve, the Blessed Virgin Mary, in her "yes" to God. (See 1 Corinthians 15:22 regarding Christ the new Adam and Luke 1:26-38 on the Annunciation; see also 2 Corinthians 5:17 and Galatians 6:15 concerning the "new creation.")

Thus we have a double kinship. First, we have a

kinship with all of humanity by virtue of our creation by God the Father. Second, we have a kinship with one another in the Church as members of the Body of Christ through baptism. This greatly enriches the "imperative of empathy" that students of grief like Sapolsky see in the universal experience of grief. We certainly agree with him that one thing we have in common with all other human beings, by virtue of our creation, is what he calls "the universal predictability" of our mourning. For Sapolsky, mourning is his connection with other human beings. It is the tie that binds. But the "imperative of empathy" for Catholics consists in the words and deeds of Jesus Christ. Through him, and through the Church, grief may become a window of opportunity for spiritual growth. It may, by God's grace, become a means of grace.

Thus it is appropriate for us to view these universal patterns as the handiwork of our heavenly Father — that is, as providential. Grief is his provision for us in the same way as our ability to understand or to make moral judgments are provisions from God for life. And interestingly, these predictable patterns seem to spontaneously organize our experience of grief. It isn't haphazard or given to chance. Since we know what to expect, we can also know the task we need to complete in order to grieve well.

Grief has a job description. In the past, Christians read books on how to die a good death. This is a book about "how to have a good grief." Good grief is an achievement from this perspective. Although one may argue that the language of "grief work" is not very pastoral, it nevertheless provides us with a useful way of knowing how we or our friends and family are doing with our grief. And it provides a way for us to bring some degree of order into a process that often feels out of control, oppressive, and chaotic.

Grief's Job Description

Grief's job description breaks down into four tasks. This is the work grief has to do in us. My discussion of these four tasks here owes much to J. William Worden's analysis in his book *Grief Counseling and Grief Therapy.*

Acceptance of the Reality of the Loss

The first task is to accept the reality of the loss. As Sapolsky points out, there is a universal human "tendency to find it hard to believe in tragedy when it strikes." Consider your reaction when you heard of the unexpected death of a celebrity: Princess Diana, John Lennon, or John Kennedy, to name but a few. Most likely, you could not believe the news, could not grasp the fact that the person was actually dead.

This is the same reaction we have when a loved one dies or when we are betrayed by a close friend — shock and disbelief. Our instinct is denial. Throughout this book we will be referring back to "denial" over and over again, since it is a foundational experience. Denial has been the fodder for jokes and even popular music recently, which shows that the concept is soaking into our popular culture. Denial is a highly complex and useful human experience, as we shall see. But the first task of grief is to break through denial.

Experiencing the Pain of the Loss

The second task for the grief-stricken person is the need to experience the pain of the loss. This is probably how most of us understand grieving. When we say that someone is "grieving," what we usually mean is that the person is experiencing the pain of grief. But the process of grief entails more than pain. In fact, the process of avoiding the pain is what we have labeled "denial."

Some old sayings common among people recovering from chemical or alcohol dependency are instructive here: "Healing comes from moving toward the pain rather than away from it." Also, "No pain, no gain." Clearly these truisms are not applicable only to substance-abuse issues. They are true for us all.

Pastors and counselors know this is troubling and uncomfortable work not only for the grieving person but for their friends and relatives as well. We tend to want to take the pain away. We want to ease the burden. But that is not what the person needs at this point, and the attempt to remove the pain may well lead to an unnecessary lengthening and deepening of the period of bereavement. What we need is to experience the pain. And often that is made possible by our friends and family who are willing to sit with us in that very difficult place.

A priest once had a parishioner who, along with her husband, had been alienated from the Church for a number of years. She was reunited with the Church following the sudden death of her husband. She literally wept through every service. Most of the people were uncomfortable with her outward display of grief to the point that they avoided her. They were not cold or unfeeling people. They simply did not know how to respond to the woman's unveiled sadness and pain. Several of the ladies were concerned enough for the woman that they spoke to the priest about it. "I don't know what to say to Bertha," one said. "When she cries, I want to cry too," offered another. The priest asked them a question: "If she can't bring her grief, all of her grief, to the altar, then where can she bring it?" "Of course," the women said. Bertha was encouraged to spend time with the other women during the week and talk about her husband. Eventually her weepiness subsided.

The point is that the pain of loss must be experienced and processed. Prolonging our avoidance of the pain of grief is not helpful and can be downright detrimental.

Adjusting to the New Environment

David Gelernter, Associate Professor of Computer Science at Yale University, had just been on a vacation in Washington visiting the museums and enjoying the Mall even though it was packed with tourists. His mail had piled up, and when he returned to his office the package on his chair caught his attention. Gelernter says that the package had a plastic zip cord.

"When I pulled the cord," he recalls, "acrid white smoke billowed out — I remember the hiss and the strange smell — and moments later, a terrific flash. My first thought was along the line of: bombs must be going off all over campus this morning. . . . I couldn't see out of my right eye, and my first thought was that I ought to wash it out, because it might have been sprayed with something that could destroy it. I traipsed to the bathroom in the middle of the building. . . . It hit me as I entered the bathroom that I was bleeding buckets and should come up with another plan."

Gelernter had set off an explosive device sent by the Unabomber. He made it out the door and was later transported to the hospital, where he was told that if he had waited to be found he probably would have died. His blood pressure in the emergency room was zero. His stay in the hospital was long and painful, and when he finally came home he found his old way of life was forever lost.

The third task of mourning is the need to adjust to an environment without the thing that is lost. We carry on our lives without the deceased loved one. After relocating, we adjust to new surroundings and people. After losing a job, we adjust to the loss of familiar tasks and colleagues. This task of adjustment can take time and has many complexities, and it usually involves considerable work.

David Gelernter describes the new world he encountered when he left the hospital: "I don't know how to confront the world one-handed and one-eyed. In the hospital I didn't need to confront it, but now I do, and there are precious few activities that don't involve clear vision and your right hand. My deep confusion is not a question of everyday tactics, it is the rest of my life: Permanent damage brings the whole rest of your life into play, pulls everything out of every closet and drawer and dumps it in a pile in front of you, and wherever you go, there is the rest-of-your-life problem to climb over. How will you do it in this suddenly modified body, with this suddenly unclear vision?"

Gelernter developed new skills and found creative ways of coping with the permanent damage that was done to him in the explosion. He could have failed to fulfill this task by simply not adjusting to the permanent loss of his sight and right hand. He could have developed dependency, helplessness, and a defeated attitude instead of rising to the challenge. But as important as our eyes and hands are, the saddest loss would have been the permanent loss of a spiritual vision for his life. Gelernter began to live life deeper and more spiritually.

Reinvesting in a New Life

The fourth task of mourning focuses upon the need to withdraw emotional energy and reinvest it in another relationship. If we are dealing with death, then the new situation may well be a new relationship with another person. If we are dealing with the loss connected to infertility, we have to let go of one dream (the dream to become pregnant and have a baby) in order to invest our life and energy in another dream (for example, adoption). A person recovering from alcohol dependency ends his old "relationship" with alcohol, knowing such a relationship leads to his moral, spiritual, and physical death. So he must reinvest in new relationships that will enhance his moral, spiritual, and physical well-being.

It is this fourth task of grieving where the potential for a new life may be realized. William Worden says that the best way to describe incompletion of this final task is "not loving." This is for many people the most difficult of all the tasks because a prerequisite to completion is the willingness to let go of the past. But the past — whether it is a dream, a person, a job, or a place — is often so cherished, and it so goes to the very heart of our identity, that the very idea of "letting go" is terrifying.

As challenging as it is, most people succeed quite well in letting go. And that opens up new relationships, occasionally in unexpected ways. We deepen as human beings. For example, David Gelernter laments his long hospital stay and absence from his two young sons. They had turned three and six around the time of the explosion. He had bought his six-year-old his first softball and mitt for his birthday. He looked forward to playing ball with his son. Now that dream was never to be. On the other hand, a new understanding and relationship with his sons began to emerge.

According to Gelernter: "What bothered me most in the hospital was that I would never be able to do that [play ball with his sons]. It still bothers me acutely. But it is possible I gained more than I lost as a father. I never had the slightest doubt that fatherhood was my most important line of work, but nowadays each of their birthdays marks another year I have succeeded in being with them and doing what I can for them, and each year is an important victory. What I want most is to live long enough to see them safely into manhood — the common hope of all parents, I guess."

The long, hard task of withdrawing emotional energy from the past and reinvesting it in the future can deepen us as we learn to move on and to love.

How the Church Grieved for Jesus

The four tasks of grieving are part of the universal pattern of how human beings deal with loss — the "catholic" nature of grief. It so happens that the Church modeled this pattern for us as she faced the loss of her founder.

Jesus wasn't planning to be around in the flesh to guide his Church into the kingdom of God, a point he makes again and again. He must go away in order for the Comforter, the Holy Spirit, to come. He tells Mary Magdalene not to cling to him — that is, not to cling to his corporeal reality. Jesus tried over and over again to prepare his disciples for his own death and eventual return to his Father. He often spoke of his need to go to Jerusalem to suffer and die.

His efforts were met with denial. His warnings seemed to go in one ear and out the other of his disciples. After Peter's profession of faith that Jesus was indeed the long-awaited Christ, the Son of the living God, this is what we are told about the passion of our Lord: "From that time Jesus began to show his disciples that he must go to Jerusalem and suffer many things from the elders and chief priest and scribes, and be killed, and on the third day be raised. And Peter took him and began to rebuke him, saying, 'God forbid, Lord! This shall never happen to you' " (Matthew 16:21-23).

Another example of the disciples not catching on or avoiding what Jesus was teaching concerning his passion is found in the Gospel of Luke: "And taking the twelve, he said to them, 'Behold, we are going up to Jerusalem, and everything that is written of the Son of man by the prophets will be accomplished. For he will be delivered to the Gentiles, and will be mocked and shamefully treated and spit upon, they will scourge him and kill him, and on the third day he will rise.' But they understood none of these things; this saying was hid from them, and they did not grasp what was said" (18:31-34).

It wasn't until after Jesus' death, resurrection, and ascension that the disciples understood what he had been talking about.

It is not stretching the point at all to say that the Apostles over and over again fell back into denial. A few passages refer to the disciples' sadness when contemplating the Lord's passion, but we get the feeling that they ignored this or put the thought out of their minds as soon as possible. After the raising of Lazarus we have the declaration of Thomas that they all should go with Jesus to Jerusalem and die with him. That, of course, was foolishness. They scattered like spiders when he was arrested. Thomas's talk of dying with the Lord seems more bravado than earnest acceptance of his passion.

But let us not be too hard on Thomas and the others. They were not slow-witted or dishonest. They were simply human, and the horror of what Jesus was telling them was too much to bear. They couldn't accept it.

The Gift of the Notorious Sinner

The event that occurred in the house of Simon the Pharisee with the woman who is referred to as "a notorious sinner" was a break with this normal pattern of denial. One day Jesus was dining with Simon the Pharisee when a woman who had a bad reputation in town burst into the dinner to see him. She crashed the party in a manner of speaking, carrying with her an alabaster box of expensive perfume. Mark tells us that the perfume would have cost a year's wages.

What she did with the perfume was astonishing. She broke the box open and poured the perfume over Jesus' head and feet. What Jesus did was even more astonishing. He simply sat there and let her do it. The strong fragrance must have been unbearable as it spread throughout the house. We actually have that interesting detail given to us by John: "The house was filled with the fragrance of the ointment" (12:3). The people at the gathering were shocked and complained about the "waste" on the one hand, and on the other hand they complained about Jesus allowing "a woman like her" to touch him at all. Specifically, it was Judas Iscariot, the treasurer of the disciples, who complained that the perfume could have been sold to feed the poor. Dubious, to say the least. And it was Simon the Pharisee who judged Jesus for allowing this sinful woman to even touch him.

But Jesus paid her one of the greatest compliments recorded in the Gospels. He said that wherever the Gospel was preached in the world, this story would be told in memory of this woman. Then Jesus himself said: "She has done what she could; she has anointed my body beforehand for the burial" (cf. John 12:7).

Sometimes words just do not have the power to express what we need to say deep down inside. We need ritual and symbolism — actions that have profound and lasting meaning for us and our community. This woman had experienced the love of God through Jesus, and it seems that she grasped what the disciples had missed. She was already experiencing the grief that would eventually rip through this little flock of believers. That this account is told from several points of view in the Gospels is evidence of its importance to the apostolic Church.

The Struggle to Accept

It is interesting to contemplate how the major feasts of our Lord mark turning points for the Church's changing relationship with him. In a way we can view her ascent through the grief process by his feast days. Holy Week expresses this exquisitely. Holy Thursday marks the beginning of Jesus' passion. On Good Friday we commemorate his death for us. We celebrate his resurrection on Easter Sunday. Then forty days later we mark his ascension. With his ascension he leaves. He goes away. He returns to his Father. Human nature is forever joined to the divine nature in the Second Person of the Trinity. The Son returned to the Father, only now he carried with him full human nature fitted for heaven. Then, ten days later, at Pentecost the Holy Spirit came upon the Church and gave her a supernatural and holy life. After Pentecost the Church was motivated to move out of Jerusalem and into the pagan world to carry the message of God's love in Jesus Christ to the whole world.

In this little summary of the beginnings of the Church we see each of the tasks of grieving. The first task is to accept the reality of the loss. In the case of the Apostles and the early Church the task was to accept the hard reality of Jesus' passion and return to his Father. Though his disciples demonstrate great difficulty in accepting this reality, the woman who anointed Jesus' feet probably grasped it. For others the biting reality dawned upon them with his arrest in the Garden of Gethsemane. For still others it was after his arrest. We are reminded of Peter's denial of any knowledge of Christ as he stood by the charcoal fire outside the courtyard of the high priest. Just as he denied Jesus the third time, the cock crowed and he looked into the courtyard. Jesus turned and their eyes met!

As Luke describes it: "And the Lord turned and looked at Peter. And Peter remembered the word of the Lord, how he had said to him, 'Before the cock crows today, you will deny me three times.' And he went out and wept bitterly" (22:61-62).

For others it may not have been until Jesus was actually nailed to the Cross that they accepted what he had been saying all along. But at some point each one of his disciples had to cross the threshold of denial into acceptance. It is like that for all of us. We all move at different paces when it comes to our willingness and ability to accept the reality of our losses. We have "a tendency to find it hard to believe in tragedy when it strikes," as Robert Sapolsky indicated earlier.

The Church in Pain

But as soon as we step into the strange new world of acceptance we enter into the second task of mourning — to experience the pain of the grief. In her ritual of anointing Jesus' head and feet with the perfume, this woman in the Gospel also embraces the pain of her grief. She wept so much that Jesus was moved to comment upon her grief in the same breath as he rebuked Simon the Pharisee: "Then turning toward the woman he said to Simon, 'Do you see this woman? I entered your house, you gave me no water for my feet, but she has wet my feet with her tears and wiped them with her hair' " (Luke 7:44).

Peter's experience, as we have seen, is instructive. He feels godly sorrow not only over his own betrayal of Jesus, but also over the realization of what is happening to Jesus. St. Luke's Gospel goes on to record that upon Peter's third denial and the crowing of the cock, the Lord turned to look at Peter, who wept unabashedly after recalling Jesus' prediction that he, Peter, would deny knowing him (cf. Luke 22:61-62).

I would suggest that Peter then entered fully into the pain of grief, that he could no longer avoid the reality of Jesus' passion. Nothing was going to be the same anymore. Remember, at this time the disciples did not know that Jesus would rise from the dead. They all scattered and hid behind locked doors to protect themselves from the authorities. From their experience the Passion meant a disastrous end to all that Jesus had done and taught over the last three years.

One might object here: But the Resurrection did

happen and that makes all the difference in the world! True, but we Christians need to work at not being too pat with our solutions to grief and loss. The Resurrection is indeed the turning point of history. We are all Christians because we believe in the resurrection of Jesus Christ, and because of the Resurrection we grieve differently from unbelievers (cf. 1 Thessalonians 4:13-15). But we grieve nonetheless.

The problem comes when we attempt to avoid the pain of acceptance by countering our feelings with the dogma of the Resurrection. "One day we'll be together after the Resurrection" and "He's in a better place" are the common pronouncements we hear from well-meaning friends at the funeral or the wake. Yes . . . but! We can move too fast here. Our faith in the Resurrection is comforting because it is true. But it doesn't remove the hard reality: *The one we have lost is not with us bodily as he or she once was.*

The disciples had this very same experience with Jesus. The accounts recorded in Scripture teach us that after his resurrection our Lord appeared to his disciples over a period of forty days and finally ascended to return to his Father. Then came another turning point for the followers of Jesus: "When they had gathered together they asked him, 'Lord, are you at this time going to restore the kingdom of Israel?' He answered them, 'It is not for you to know the times or seasons that the Father has established by his own authority. But you will receive power when the Holy Spirit comes upon you, and you will be my witnesses in Jerusalem, throughout Judea and Samaria, and to the ends of the earth.' When he had said this, as they were looking on, he was lifted up, and a cloud took him from their sight" (Acts 1:6-9, NAB).

The disciples still didn't get it! They asked Jesus if he planned to restore the kingdom to Israel at this point.

In other words they were not even close to letting go of him. They wanted Jesus to stay and lead them on to God's victory now. They were having real problems imagining, much less accepting, what their lives would be like without these occasional appearances of their resurrected Lord. They were still doing what Mary Magdalene had attempted in the burial garden when Jesus said to her: "Stop holding on to me, for I have not yet ascended to the Father" (John 20:17, NAB).

The Church Accepts and Adjusts

The third task of mourning has to do with making the necessary adjustments to live in the new world bereft of the person or some other significant relationship in our lives. For the disciples this meant living in the world without the bodily presence of our Lord to lead, guide, comfort, and teach them. (The Real Presence of our Lord in the Eucharist is another example of having to relate to him differently.)

The final task of the mourner, as mentioned earlier, is to withdraw emotional energy and reinvest it in another relationship. Christians cannot understand this to mean that we stop loving the person who is dead. We believe in the communion of saints, who are still participating members of the Body of Christ. We don't stop loving a person because he or she isn't around us anymore. Much of this is a matter of striking a balance. If we are so emotionally involved with the loss that we cannot invest time and emotional energy in new relationships, then a problem exists. We become stuck. We cannot move forward. And it is important to note that reinvestment in another relationship doesn't necessarily mean another relationship of the kind we have lost. What is important is the ability and desire to reenter life and relationships.

The Church's relationship with our Lord is instructive in this task. As Peter writes to the first generation of Christians after the Ascension, "Without having seen him you love him" (1 Peter 1:8). One clear mark of apostolic Christianity is the ardent love that the disciples of the following generations had for Jesus Christ, even though they had never experienced him bodily in the same way that the Apostles had. For us, then, it seems that "to withdraw emotional energy and reinvest it in another relationship" is best understood as not clinging to the past. Because of our belief in the communion of saints and prayers for the departed, we understand that we are in relationship with them, albeit different from what it was before death.

The critical test for the Christian is the ability to reinvest in a new relationship. Once again the Scriptures are instructive. Let us look at a well-known account of the crucifixion: "But standing by the cross of Jesus were his mother, and his mother's sister, Mary the wife of Clopas, and Mary Magdalene. When Jesus saw his mother, and the disciple whom he loved standing near, he said to his mother, 'Woman, behold, your son!' Then he said to the disciple, 'Behold, your mother!' And from that hour the disciple took her to his own home" (John 19:25-27).

In this account, our Lord himself takes the initiative to move both his mother and the disciple into a new relationship. This new relationship was made possible only by our Lord's passion, crucifixion, death, resurrection, ascension, and the coming of the Holy Spirit (Pentecost), each of which changed his relationship to the Church. The new relationship between Jesus and the Church was made even more clear by the Ascension and Pentecost. If anything the Passion, the Ascension, and Pentecost made a plethora of new relationships possible within the Church. Our Lord's return to his Father in heaven made possible relationships with the Holy Spirit, with the Apostles, with the Blessed Virgin, and with the saints.

So we can see in the early life of the Church how the individual disciples and the Church as a whole not only went through this process of grief but also made the appropriate adjustments in their relationship to our Lord and to the new situation created by his passion and crucifixion, resurrection, ascension, and Pentecost. The point for us who are living at the dawning of the third millennium is that Catholics continue to live with loss in much the same way as our matriarchs and patriarchs and the Apostles did two thousand years ago. Grief is the way our experiences of loss are spontaneously organized. Bereavement is an opportunity for growth when we make the appropriate adjustments in our relationships to the new life. Whether we are grieving the loss of a loved one, the loss of a significant dream, or any of the myriad of losses we go through in life, certain experiences are predictable and certain tasks help us to keep moving in a healthy and wholesome direction. Let us now turn our attention to the experience of grief itself.

3 The Many Faces of Denial

A few years ago I realized that I was having problems reading the text of the Mass while at the altar. I made excuses: "I was tired"; "I was distracted"; "I'm overworked"; "I wasn't working out enough" or "I was working out too much." Finally, an ophthalmologist in my parish watched me fumble with the text and asked me to stop by his office for an examination. I now use reading glasses like millions of other middle-aged men do, and the problem is solved.

It was a small but revealing example of denial. A problem was growing in my life — a nagging, embarrassing question with painful implications. For many months I wasn't even aware of the problem. I did not let it intrude into my consciousness. When I could no longer fully deny the issue, I made excuses. In the end, with professional help, I had to break through the layers of denial and confront the painful truth: My vision was impaired.

This incident caused me some embarrassment. But

denial can be more far-reaching and damaging, particularly for people experiencing a traumatic loss. My friend Father Bob told me one such sad story.

Upon arrival at the airport Father Bob phoned a couple we will call Jim and Wanda White. He had become close to the White family in his former parish and he took this opportunity to visit with them while on his way to a workshop. Father Bob had not seen the Whites in several years. He had grown especially close to the family after their son, Robbie, had drowned at a church camp six years previously. He wanted to see how they were doing.

Jim and Wanda were thrilled to have their former young priest over and invited him to spend the night. Much of the evening Jim and Wanda spoke of Robbie as if he were still alive. They showed Father Bob to his room. It was actually Robbie's former room, and what struck Father Bob was that it was almost a shrine to Robbie. His parents had left the room completely intact since his death. The books on the bureau and the fishing pole in the corner were right where he had left them. The whole night was spent focused upon Robbie. Father Bob came to realize that the Whites had never accepted the reality of the loss of their son. They continued to live in the past.

Grief unfolds in stages. The best-known theory of the stages of grief was advanced by Elisabeth Kübler-Ross in 1969 in her groundbreaking book. In studying terminally ill patients and their families, Dr. Kübler-Ross found that both the patients and their families went through certain predictable experiences. She thought it followed a pattern and sequence: denial, anger, bargaining, depression, and acceptance. This scheme is useful, but one ought not to view it too rigidly. These are not precise stages — as in the development of an embryo; instead, they are softer, more flexible, and less exact. Think of them in terms of the weather and the seasons.

Daily variations in temperature and rainfall are hard to predict, but the general pattern is fairly clear. Winter gives way to spring, and summer eventually comes around. But we know that fall and winter will return — maybe mild, maybe icy.

Pastors and health care workers know from experience that people move back and forth between these "stages" as they work through them. And a large part of pastoral care of the grieving is understanding how the larger patterns of grief should work. In my view, the process of grief involves surmounting three challenges: (1) shock and/or denial, (2) feelings, and (3) mapping and making a new life.

Jim and Wanda White are stuck in the first one: denial.

Denial can look peculiar and odd to outsiders — even funny. There is a great scene about denial in the movie *Moonstruck*, starring Nicholas Cage and Cher. Cher plays a woman who has become engaged to the brother of the character played by Nicholas Cage. The engagement is not especially an enthusiastic one from Cher's point of view, and Cage has fallen madly and hopelessly in love with her. They are talking in the bakery where Cage works. The conversation is emotionally charged. Cage is running on about his love for her and all his problems in life. Suddenly, Cher gives him a big slap across the face and shouts: "Snap out of it!" And to some degree, for the moment, he does snap out of it.

The scene is sad and funny because it taps into our impatience with people who are in denial. One of the hallmarks of denial is that the person in denial cannot see it; but everyone else can — that is, *usually* everyone else can. There is such a thing as systemic denial. Sometimes a whole system — a family, a community, a parish — collectively participates in and sustains the denial of some significant reality. Something like this was the case with the Apostles themselves. The fairy tale of the emperor's new clothes is about systemic denial.

Like one of those tricky extraterrestrials in the *Star Trek* movies who is always morphing into something else, changing its appearance, so denial has many faces. Once again we will rely upon J. William Worden and his work in grief therapy. Worden cites five ways that people practice denial: (1) denying the facts of the loss, (2) denying the meaning of the loss, (3) selective forgetting, (4) denying the irreversibility of the loss, and (5) spiritualism.

Denying the Facts of the Loss

Denying the facts of the loss is something that we all practice to one degree or another. We don't *see* what has happened. We push the facts of the situation beyond our consciousness. I did this as my eyesight weakened. Frequently, denying the facts can reach dangerous and extreme proportions.

Jennifer P. Schneider in her book *Back from Betrayal* tells the story of a forty-four-year-old lawyer named Gillian, who had met her husband when they were both in college. Gillian was attracted to her handsome husband because "he had a lot of problems and he needed to be taken care of." He went to medical school and she stayed home. They had several children. He had several affairs, and he was frequently absent from home. Gillian pretended she didn't know about his affairs. She was also out of touch with the reality of his inattentiveness to her and their children.

One day she walked in on her husband while he was in a compromising position with a nurse. That changed everything. Until then she had pretended that everything was OK. She was crushed emotionally. Denial had allowed her to tolerate an intolerable and potentially dangerous situation for years. Once the veil of illusion was rent, Gillian had to make some very difficult decisions and she was thrust headlong into the pain of grief.

The capacity that human beings have for denying the facts of a loss is immense and varied. How many times have we denied warnings that we have a physical problem or sickness? We suffer a loss, and pretend that nothing has changed.

Denying the Meaning of the Loss

Denial is sometimes experienced by denying the *meaning* of the loss. We convince ourselves that it doesn't have the significance others think it does — in fact, it does. Understanding and acknowledging reality is sometimes a slippery matter, but facts are facts. As in all forms of denial, the reality emerges in some form and often in uncharacteristic ways and unexpected places, even when we wish it would not.

Those ways and places may be destructive as in the case of Julie, a lovely young college woman who had entered a psychiatric hospital for depression. Julie had been a bright psychology major in a state university. Within a year, she had gone to pieces. She had become entangled with a man who physically abused her. She started drinking and staying out late at night. Her grades plummeted and she dropped out of school. All of this behavior was completely out of character for Julie, who had always loved school and set high standards and goals for herself.

Upon entering the hospital she was placed in a grief group. After several days of work in the group, with the members telling their life stories, Julie's problem began to emerge. Her life had been very happy except for one incident that had occurred about a year and a half earlier. Her childhood home had burned to the ground while she was away at college. Julie had wanted to come home, but her parents were not injured in the fire, so they encouraged her to stay at school — even though she was only a four-hour drive away. Julie had a very strong attachment to the house that had burned down. Her parents had kept her room for her just as she had left it and she lived in it during the summer months when school was not in session. Much of her identity and meaning was attached to the house, the same one her mother had grown up in. Julie's childhood and the family's history were, in more ways than one, part of that house. When the fire occurred, nothing was saved. Her parents had been away at the time. All the artifacts of her personal history had gone up in flames.

When Julie did return home after an unhappy semester, she found that the remains of the house had been razed and a new home was going up on the site of the old one. All that was left was some scorched ground. Julie recognized her loss, but denied that it had intense personal meaning. Then her personal disintegration and depression began.

When Julie finally acknowledged just how much her home had meant to her, she had a breakthrough. But that took a lot of hard work on her part. The home wasn't a person, and so she even felt a little guilty for feeling so sad about losing it. She began her work in the grief group by saying her life had been perfect and nothing bad had ever happened to her. The house, she said at first, "didn't mean that much to me. Anyway, the new home is a lot nicer and I don't miss the old one." This minimizing of the loss is the way Julie was denying its full meaning.

Selective Forgetting

Selective forgetting is the third method of denial. Sometimes the happiest times may be too painful to remember. People will sometimes unrealistically elevate the relationship with the lost loved one. There is a sort of deification that selectively glosses over characteristics that are painful to deal with. What occasionally happens is that the grieving process is short-circuited by putting the person on a pedestal and ignoring that individual's shortcomings. Anytime a person is put on a pedestal we tend to ignore parts of his or her reality. We shrink from the truth because the truth is painful. We know that real people are not divine, but human and flawed like us. Occasionally selective forgetting can become extreme.

William Worden cites the example of a young man who lost his father in childhood. The memory of losing his father was so painful that over the years he blocked his father's memory from his conscious thoughts. He even forgot what he looked like until he went through therapy in college. When he graduated he said that he sensed his father's presence, something that would have been impossible before facing his denial.

I have known siblings who would argue over a parent's behavior years after the parent's death. It is interesting how the birth sequence of the children and their memory of a parent differ. The "baby" may recall a parent who was affectionate and always there, while the firstborn recalls a distant parent who never had enough time for him. Granted, parents grow during the process of parenting children, but this shows how complex our memories of our families are. It also shows that "selective forgetting" and "selective remembering" goes on all the time. One of the best ways to help people with this problem is to listen to them patiently. It may take some time, as with the young man Worden cited; but patient, loving listening will provide the setting for enabling such individuals to recall what is repressed.

The Denial of the Irreversibility of Death

A fourth way in which we deny reality is to deny the irreversibility of death. Whether it is the loss of a dream, the loss of youth, the loss of a relationship, or the loss of a loved one through death, we sometimes get stuck with the notion that it can all be fixed — that the reality can be reversed. It is not uncommon for the grieving survivors to be plagued by the fantasy that the dead loved one is still alive somewhere, perhaps is about to walk into the room. This is normal, but the fantasy can have a terrible hold on the affected person.

Jim and Wanda were probably mired in this form of denial as their life continued to revolve around their son, Robbie, six years dead. I recall reports of several mothers and fathers who had lost children and family in a Burma air crash staying at the crash site for days "praying for a miracle." They hoped that their loved ones had been thrown free of the crash or would literally rise from the dead. Such scenes are poignant and touch our hearts. These experiences tend to demonstrate the human capacity to deny the reality of the loss even in the face of overwhelming evidence.

Good pastoral care, indeed good Christian friendship, will not scold the bereaved for expressing natural human feelings and hopes. But we also need to plan on being around when the prayers of the faithful are answered in ways that they would want to deny. A ministry of presence at moments like this is the most powerful. Words are forgotten, theological explanations are set aside. What is remembered is that we were not alone. Our friends in the Church were there for us and with us. That is incarnational theology.

Spiritualism and Over-Spiritualizing

Worden calls the fifth way of denial "spiritualism." Again, for our purposes here as Catholics, we need to refine this a bit and then add to it. Spiritualism is the unchristian practice of attempting to make contact with the dead and to achieve some form of reunion with them.

It is specifically forbidden for Christians and Jews to participate in such practices (cf. Leviticus 19:31 and 20:6, 27; Deuteronomy 18:12). This would include the older practice of holding séances and the New Age practice of "channeling."

The *Catechism of the Catholic Church* declares: "All forms of *divination* are to be rejected: recourse to Satan or demons, conjuring up the dead or other practices falsely supposed to 'unveil' the future [cf. *Deut* 18:10; *Jer* 29:8]. Consulting horoscopes, astrology, palm reading, interpretation of omens and lots, the phenomena of clairvoyance, and recourse to mediums all conceal a desire for power over time, history, and, in the last analysis, other human beings, as well as a wish to conciliate hidden powers. They contradict the honor, respect, and loving fear that we owe to God alone" (No. 2116).

People who practice "spiritualism" are deceived concerning their communication with the departed. Many of the early Church Fathers concluded that people who thought they were communicating with the departed were communicating with demons. One way to view the practice of necromancy is that it is a distortion of the doctrine of the communion of saints and of the virtue of hope. We pray for the blessed departed, and we believe that they pray for us, but New Age attempts to communicate directly with them are deceitful.

We also have to make a distinction between "spiritualism" and the practice of many Christians of "over-spiritualizing." The Church has very specific beliefs about those who "sleep in Christ." Among those beliefs is that spiritual growth doesn't stop with death. Thus we pray for the "whole state of Christ's Church," and we pray for the growth in grace of our loved ones who are with the Lord.

But the Church also teaches us that death is a reality that separates us from the space-time continuum we perceive ourselves to be presently living in. Death is a hard reality — even in a Christian context where the Resurrection takes a good deal of the sting away. It helps us not to fall into despair and view life as a futile, short, and painful experience that ends once and for all with our physical demise. But even in the face of the blessed hope of everlasting life, the fact of the matter is that we do not in this present moment have our departed loved ones with us — just as the Apostles no longer had Jesus with them bodily. We believe that we shall rise from the dead and we will be reunited with our loved ones. But Christians must be careful not to jump to the spiritual answer too quickly. We need to be careful not to use Catholic truth as a way to avoid the reality and the pain of the loss.

There is a lovely account in the Acts of the Apostles that illustrates this point. St. Paul had been in Ephesus for three years teaching and establishing the Church in that region. He had a difficult time of it, but he had grown very close to the people in the Church in Ephesus. Then it was time for him to move on and establish more parishes. When he was ready to depart, he sent word to the priests and leaders to meet him by the sea where he was ready to sail. There he spoke of his love for them and reminisced about what they had accomplished together over that three-year period. He gave them warnings not to depart from the orthodox, apostolic faith. When he had finished, there was hardly a dry eye among them. Luke sums up the account with these words: "When he had finished speaking he knelt down and prayed with them all. They were all weeping loudly as they threw their arms around Paul and kissed him, for they were deeply distressed that he had said that they would never see his face again. Then they escorted him to the ship" (Acts 20:36-38, NAB).

The pathos of this account still moves the reader. It

is so honest. Clearly these people believed they would see Paul's face again — in heaven. But the likelihood of seeing him again in this life was indeed small. They knew that Paul was a man with a mission from God and that he would not rest until he had burned himself out for the Lord. They were saying good-bye to him for the last time and they knew it. The Resurrection makes all the difference in the world, but the sadness for the loss in this present time is just as real.

Respect Denial

Before we leave the topic of denial we need to say just a word about the need to have the proper respect for denial. Even though we have concentrated largely upon the negative aspects of denial, there are positive ones as well. Denial plays a critical role in the grieving process and for that reason we need to respect it. Gerald May, a therapist who has published much concerning spiritual issues and recovery, has pointed out that denial may, "on a temporary and expedient basis, provide us with time and energy to secure ourselves in other areas of life and thereby build up enough courage to turn around and face reality" *(Addiction and Grace)*.

Denial isn't evil; rather, it is a first response to the loss. In a manner of speaking it is a sort of safety device, an emotional air bag, that protects us from the potentially overwhelming emotions associated with the loss. Just as an air bag in our automobiles inflates upon impact and cushions the passenger from being crushed, so denial cushions the crush of emotions crashing in upon us at the moment of our loss. Denial viewed this way is a provision of the Creator who is always sustaining us.

It is important to realize that people cannot be pushed out of denial. Nor should we attempt to push them. The person who is in denial concerning a major loss is in the process of shoring up his or her life against chaos and destruction. No wonder people get stuck.

For Gillian, the lawyer whose physician-husband was chronically unfaithful, it was not merely her "relationship" with her husband that kept her in denial. She had her family to think about. The children's education and health, their standing in the community, and the family's life itself, as well as her own wishes and dreams — all of these helped hold her in place, allowing her to hope against hope. For the Whites it was a matter of facing the shattering reality of life without their son.

For the Apostles and disciples it was a matter of accepting the new reality that the Messiah would reign from a cross rather than a throne in Jerusalem. Their whole culture had taught them that the Messiah would drive back the pagans and establish Israel's rule. The Apostles quite naturally experienced denial during our Lord's earthly ministry when he began to hint to them that he would have to suffer for the sins of the world. It is easy to see how their denial actually aided them. What would have happened if they had absorbed the truth of what he was saying at the very beginning? At least one possibility is that his impending passion might have loomed so large in their thoughts that they would have been paralyzed by it. At any rate the point is that denial is not necessarily unhealthy. In fact, it is needed in our lives, as long as we don't continue on in denial beyond an appropriate time.

Denial and Dependency

Denial is a major contributor to alcohol and chemical dependency. Gerald May points out that self-deception is one of the major traits of denial: "During the early stages of the development of chemical addiction, the conscious mind studiously ignores or rejects any signs of increasing use of the substance. Not only does the person not recognize that a problem exists, she doesn't want to think about it. She doesn't see any reason to consider it. This is denial" *(Addiction and Grace)*.

Seriously troubled grief-and-loss experiences are frequently at the root of alcoholism, eating disorders, sex addiction, and chemical dependency. A psychologist I know who works in the area of grief and loss once cited a typical example for me. He conducted a seminar for other professionals who presented case studies of people with chemical-dependency issues and eating disorders. In eight of the ten cases he diagnosed that the person was suffering from a chronic grief disorder. The people in the case studies were using the chemicals or alcohol to deal with the pain of grief. To further complicate matters, once such people enter recovery programs, they must deal with grief over the loss of the alcohol or whatever it was they had become dependent upon. For many people, giving up alcohol or an eating disorder was compared to losing their best friend.

The model for dealing with denial and dependency is the twelve-step program developed by Alcoholics Anonymous. Twelve-step recovery programs can be found for overeaters and those dependent on drugs and alcohol — even for people who spend too freely and specific issues such as "women who love too much"!

But the application of the twelve steps to other issues has caused suspicion on the part of many people. Indeed, there are certainly examples of the misuse of the twelve-step idea and the idea of "recovering communities." But often clichés and slogans remain superficial only because we approach them superficially. When you begin to take what may appear to be clichés seriously and attempt to live them out, they suddenly become true to life and not so easily dismissed.

Such is the case, I believe, with AA. The slogans like "One day at a time" actually have a spiritually rich background to them and they work if they are implemented. One reason they work is that AA was originally founded within a very specific Christian context; therefore, these principles of living have the Christian faith for their source. (See, for example, Matthew 6 and 7, 1 Peter 5:5-9, and Philippians 4:6-7.) Bill Wilson, the founder of AA, had his last drink on December 11, 1934. He had just been introduced to Father Samuel Shoemaker, an Anglican priest who was running Calvary Mission in New York City. Later, Wilson took lengthy instruction from Bishop Fulton Sheen, but he never converted to Roman Catholicism. Wilson never allowed AA to be identified with any Church or denomination, but he did state plainly that the twelve steps were, in his phrase, a "spiritual kindergarten."

One thing Father Shoemaker attempts in his books is a presentation of the principles of living Christian faith in practical and doable terms. That is exactly what AA attempts to do with the twelve steps, except that all references to the Christian faith have been removed. Their reason for removing specific references to Christ had to do with their narrow and precise goal, which was to help alcoholics become sober and stay sober. For that reason they sought to broaden the message as much as possible. Many recovering alcoholics are Catholics, and many agnostics and atheists become Christians through a serious attempt to live by the twelve steps. People become better people in general through what many have viewed as a sort of Christian rule for life made available even to unbelievers, which was the original intention. Because of its origins in and among Christians, the benefits to Catholics are outstanding.

Edward Dowling, S.J., an early friend of the "fathers" of AA had this to say in the Big Book (the AA bible): "Alcoholics Anonymous is natural; it is natural at the point where nature comes closest to the supernatural, namely in humiliations and in consequent humility. There is something spiritual about an art museum or a symphony, and the Catholic Church approves of our use of them. There is something spiritual about A.A. too, and Catholic participation in it almost invariably results in poor Catholics becoming better Catholics."

One of the major issues for the alcoholic and his or her family, it was discovered, was facing the truth about the alcoholic's addiction. In other words, denial was the fundamental problem that alcoholics had to deal with and move beyond in order to begin their journey on the road to recovery. The very first step speaks directly to the issue of denial: "We admitted we were powerless over alcohol — that our lives had become unmanageable." Denial is the first and foremost major inhibitor to the acceptance of "powerlessness." The idea of powerlessness is insulting to most of us. We want to view ourselves as "in control" and "competent" in our lives. From a Christian point of view the experience of powerlessness corresponds to our state of being without Christ. It is the "admission" of our powerlessness that indicates a break from the practice of denial.

4 Feelings and Recovery

One unmistakable element of grief is strong feelings. After the initial shock and denial we are usually flooded with emotions. This is our second signpost as we travel the way of grief.

"How can I have all these feelings?" is a question that social workers and priests often hear in their offices when they are counseling people in grief. After the initial numbness passes, we experience a cascade of feelings that may last intensely from a few days to months, depending on the loss. Obviously the more significant the loss the longer and the more intense is this experience. Personal, social, and spiritual resources also play a big role in helping us integrate the loss into our lives and live with the pain. The particular emotions that one feels are amazing: sadness, anger, listlessness, rage, guilt, depression, betrayal (by the loved one, doctors, companions, and even God), agony, shame, remorse, hostility, resentment, disloyalty, devotion, relief, freedom, comfort, forgiveness, and peace. This list clearly does not exhaust the possibilities, but it shows what a wild ride grief can be emotionally.

However, emotions are not simply something we feel. Emotions are windows of perception and may become channels of communication. We naturally feel the emotion of fear when we are in a dangerous situation. Likewise, when we pick up on anger or annoyance in a person's voice we understand that something is bothering that person. The woman who anointed Jesus with expensive perfume was in the throes of sadness over her own sin and his impending death. Those feelings were reflections not only of her internal emotional state, they were also windows of perception that opened onto objective reality — in this case her sorrow over sin and the Lord's passion.

Face the Pain

One of the clear messages from grief professionals over the years has been that we need to "move toward the pain, not away from it." Denial is avoidance and the attempt to move away from pain. But healing and health come by entering fully into the pain of the loss.

Julie, the student who had lost her sense of self following the fiery destruction of her childhood home, is a good example here. She avoided the pain of the loss by reconstructing a false self. She began acting out in ways that were completely uncharacteristic of her. She began to drink a lot. She found a boyfriend who was unfaithful and abusive. She almost flunked out of school, all of which was completely atypical for Julie, who had always loved school and who had healthy relationships with boys. She couldn't face the pain of the loss of her home, and the opportunity to grieve with her family was shut down when her parents discouraged her from coming home after the fire. She missed out on the family's grief and the family decisions to rebuild on the old site.

All of this was literally like a death for her. She moved away from the healthy, authentic pain and she began moving toward a much more painful, false life. Much of Julie's pain took the form of anger at God. This was the first real tragedy she had experienced in life and she blamed God for it.

Once she had established trust in her grief group in the hospital, she started opening up little by little. Finally, she had gathered enough strength and courage to move into the pain of the loss. She began to grieve and she rediscovered the "old Julie," as her mother put it. Julie's group encouraged her to take some time and write a letter to God, honestly expressing all her feelings, even the feelings of anger and betrayal. When she had accomplished that work she experienced reconciliation with God and the Church. Her anger seemed to evaporate as she realized that God had not abandoned her, that he was with her even in this scorching experience.

The Trouble with Feelings

It is important to remember that feelings are neither good nor bad — they simply are. Behavior is something else. We Christians often have trouble with feelings because we seem to think that to feel something is morally equivalent to acting on the feelings. That isn't the case. This misunderstanding may arise from a faulty understanding of Jesus' teachings like the one presented in the Sermon on the Mount. We have heard in sermons for years how Jesus set a higher standard for the Church than is contained in the Old Testament Law.

The specific passage is found in Matthew 5:20-48. Let us take, for example, a portion of this passage: "You have heard that it was said to the men of old, 'You shall not kill; and whoever kills shall be liable to judgment.' But I say to you that every one who is angry with his brother shall be liable to judgment; whoever insults his brother shall be liable to the council, and whoever says, 'You fool!' shall be liable to the hell of fire" (5:21-22).

Bad exegesis of this passage of Scripture has led to a lot of unnecessary angst in people's lives. Priests and counselors have all had to deal with Catholics who think that somehow their feelings of anger toward a person, living or dead, are wicked. Feelings don't kill people. What is often afoot here is magical thinking that makes a correspondence between one's feelings and events. Besides that, St. Paul clearly gives a place to anger in the life of the Body of Christ. If Scripture helps to interpret Scripture, then we have to understand our Lord to be referring to something other than natural, everyday anger. What one does with his or her feelings, and that includes the decision to nurse them into characteristics of one's soul, is the critical issue.

We really can't choose the feelings we are going to have at any one moment, but we can and must decide what we will act on. Feelings aren't turned off and on in our lives like a light switch. We really have little control over the feelings that enter into our minds and hearts.

On the other hand we do have control over our behavior. We can control what we do with the feelings. We can nurse anger into hate and resentment. We can nurse lust into adultery. But we seemingly have little control over the first thought or feeling that enters into our consciousness. There is an old German saying attributed to Martin Luther: "You can't stop the birds from flying around your head, but you don't have to let them build a nest in your hair." Feelings are like that. Try as we may, we will not rid ourselves of normal feelings like sadness and anger, particularly when we experience major losses in our lives. What we have to do is to honor the feelings — to be honest with ourselves, with God, and at least with one other person. To come clean. And by all means not to act out in a destructive manner.

There is a progression in the passage of Scripture that we have quoted above. We begin with a feeling, in this case anger. But this is not really a feeling as we have been discussing it. Rather it seems to be a feeling that has become a state of being. Jesus is talking about anger with another person that has been nurtured into hatred. That state of being that leads to overt action, in this case name-calling. But not simply name-calling. It is name-calling that places the individual who is hated outside the saved community. Thus this passage has to do with the way we should live with one another within the Church. Later we will look into how Christians can relate in an honest and healthy manner to the feelings of sadness, anger, and guilt from a biblical perspective.

Feelings simply *are*. Behavior has to be subject to the law of love.

Catholic Christians, like other people, have often beaten themselves up emotionally because of what they believe to be inappropriate feelings over a loss. But what sets us Catholic Christians apart is our belief in the healing and restoring possibilities in the sacraments. The New Testament puts it this way: "If we say, 'We have fellowship with him,' while we continue to walk in darkness, we lie and do not act in truth. But if we walk in the light as he is in the light, then we have fellowship with one another, and the blood of his Son Jesus cleanses us from all sin" (1 John 1:6-7, NAB).

The possibility of "union" with one another, and that includes family members, is based upon Calvary. If there is unfinished business between the one we have lost and ourselves, then anger and guilt may be a part of that experience. It will simply do us no good to deny it. Nor will it do us any good to scold ourselves for having the "wrong" feelings about the person or the event. There are no "wrong" feelings. There are wrong actions. But we are responsible to make sure that we don't act out in a destructive or sinful way and use our feelings as an excuse. Feelings are always understandable; inappropriate and sinful behavior is not. Again all of this is simply part of the pain of the loss. It is essential to the grieving process. There is no way around it. We must enter into to it. We must go through it. But we don't have to go through it alone.

Telling the Story

One way to move toward the pain and enter into it rather than away from it is to tell the story. That is why people who have experienced a major loss usually talk about it so much. There is a need to go over the account repeatedly. The story has to be told over and over again. What is needed here is someone to listen. In the Appendix we have included guidance about forming a grief group in your parish. There is really no better context in which to tell your story than the Body of Christ.

Telling our story is sometimes very difficult. Long ago the Psalmist sang: "Deep calls to deep" (Psalm 42:7). He wasn't thinking about storytelling, but the concept expressed here can be applied to that experience. It takes time to build trust and courage to enter into what may well be threatening territory. When we begin to remember — that is, when we begin to put into words, and images, and metaphors our experience of what we have lost — it tends to be very painful at first. Tears and occasionally even sobbing are part of the experience. What is especially useful is to have another warm, caring person to listen to us. Our story of loss will often bring up other people's feelings about their own losses in life.

Sometimes this can be very powerful and specific. The members of Julie's grief-and-loss group listened to her with empathy and care. Several of them wept with Julie. And Julie's accounts, which she told repeatedly over a two-week period, helped break the ice for others to begin similar work. "Deep calls to deep." We cannot listen with care and love without being reminded of our own losses. But pastors and friends also have to use discernment about when, where, how, and if we should share that with a person we are in a helping relationship with.

I cannot emphasize one point too much: The story of our loss has to be told in a warm, accepting environment, and told repeatedly.

Mapping and Making a New Life

The last signpost of the grief experience points us in the direction of mapping and making a new life. Breaking through denial and entering into the pain of the loss clears the path for making a new life. A basic assumption of this book is that this pilgrimage is one that includes traveling companions from the Body of Christ. Isolation after a loss can lead to complicated grief, including physical and psychiatric illness. Members of strong, close families and parishes move back into life faster and in a healthier way than those who are isolated. But life once reentered will be different from the way of life before the loss.

Nancy Wartik, widely published in the field of counseling, puts it well: "Recovery from grief doesn't mean a resumption of life exactly as it was, however. Just as a deep wound leaves a bodily scar, emotional scar tissue is permanent, even when a person has moved on to a new life or love. From time to time over the years, the scar will ache. Yet many people deeply touched by grief change in remarkably positive ways. They develop new empathy for others who suffer loss or learn to deal more effectively with people or situations" (*American Health,* May 1996).

A priest in the Deep South was once paying a visit

to a member of his parish. He sat out on the front porch of an old wood-framed farmhouse with the aged widow-farmer. They drank iced tea. They talked about the corn that was chest-high and deep green. After a while she began to talk about her grief. Her husband once farmed the acres and acres of corn that stretched in front of them. That was literally decades ago. He used mules back then to break up the red clay fields. Those same fields now were nearly ripe for the harvest. Tears filled the woman's eyes as she talked about her husband and their life together on the farm. Her tears were fresh, and yet he had been dead for over thirty years. She had long since become the keeper of the farm, a member of the parish council, and a volunteer in the local hospice. She had never remarried and yet she had long since reentered life without her beloved husband. There was still hurt and pain — not constant but like the scar Wartik speaks about. Yet her reentry was robust in time and stretched her far beyond her roles and self-understanding before the loss. Childless, she was the one in her parish everyone felt safe with. She had a big heart and a natural, comfortable empathy for people who were suffering.

Reality Testing

After a loss we tend to retreat a bit as we go through the grief process. But the job isn't over until we reenter life, develop new relationships, and find new and creative ways to live without what we have lost. Reentry is not easy. And yet it is paradoxically true that we have to be easy on ourselves and others during this period. There is enough stress already. And being intentional about taking it easy and taking it one day at a time will enhance successful and creative recovery. Feelings tend to add to our stress unless they are honestly and openly dealt with. Having a close friend, a priest, or a professional counselor can be especially helpful when it comes to dealing with strange feelings like survivor's guilt and feelings of disloyalty. If we can be truthful with God, ourselves, and at least one other person, we can get through this. Another person can help us do some reality testing on the feelings we have. When we have developed trusting relationships with at least one other person it is helpful to simply ask for feedback from that person concerning some of the strange feelings we go through.

Ben had been a professor of English at a small Southern college for over fifteen years. When he lost his job in a major restructuring of the school, he was thrust into depression over the loss of something he truly loved — teaching literature. Ben discovered that much of his identity was tied up with teaching. He sent out literally over a hundred applications and résumés, only to be disappointed over and over again. Everyone wanted people who had published books and articles, but Ben had quit publishing years before and dedicated himself to teaching English literature to undergraduates. It took nearly two years without full-time work for Ben finally to admit that his chances of landing a position at a college were dreadfully dim. "If I'm not an English professor, then what am I?" he asked himself.

With the help of a supportive wife and several understanding fellow parishioners, Ben began looking for jobs outside the teaching field. He eventually went to work for a high-tech medical company as a writer. He is making more money than he used to and he enjoys his work. English literature has become his avocation. He teaches in an adult education program that the diocese has set up in his parish.

Detachment Is a Good Word

At this point in the process of recovery, "detachment" is a basic need. The word "detachment" sometimes sounds harsh and cold to people. It isn't. Detachment is necessary for making a new life because we have to let go of the loss. We have to let go and let God, as the saying in AA goes, in order to move our lives forward. Detachment is the ability to experience our feelings, to affirm the reality of the loss (its absolute nature in this life anyway), and to consciously and intentionally use our personal skills and resources — our family, our parish, and our Christian beliefs — to let go of the loss and embrace the present and the future.

This obviously cannot be pushed upon people. Detachment comes toward the end of the process and takes time to ripen. In the same way that Julie needed a safe place to take time to gather strength and courage to face the truth about the loss of her home, so detachment comes about most easily in supportive, safe environments. Detachment doesn't mean that we don't care or love anymore; it means we are conscious and intentional about living with the present reality in the light of all our strengths: personal, social, and spiritual.

The Family as a Resource

We will deal with the special spiritual resources and strengths of Catholics later. Here I want to consider the role of the family — one of the greatest resources we have available to us as we deal with loss.

The family is our original community. There we learn to trust and talk in order to express our needs and wants. The family is the place where we can be encouraged, challenged, and held accountable. The family can be a safe harbor that we return to time and again through our lives as we explore the wider world. The family can be a refuge from all the hassles and tensions that are simply a part of life.

Of course, that is not always the case. The language and insights of the recovery movement have enriched our vocabulary and understanding of how families can break down and become less constructive in our lives. We have all heard of "dysfunctional families." The phrase and its concepts have entered our popular culture through TV, movies, and a spate of manuals on the subject. A dysfunctional family is one that damages its members. The members exist for the maintenance of the family. If a family member threatens the balance of the family, that person may be brought in line in order to maintain the status quo of the family. Exaggerated senses of loyalty, guilt, and shame are often used in such families as methods of control. Members may become frozen into "roles" they play that help maintain the balance. Denial is the mainstay of dysfunctional families.

Although the concept of "family systems" is only a few decades old, the realities that lie behind it are well-rooted in our history. The novelist William Faulkner was once asked if he read the Bible. He replied that he read the Old Testament because he loved the stories about the battling families. Terms like "dysfunctional family" may only be a few years old, but it only takes one reading of the story of David or Jacob and Esau to see that dysfunctional families have been around for a long time. The dysfunctional families in the Pentateuch have problems strikingly similar to contemporary families' problems.

Family Roles

The family role is a way to minimize the challenges to the family denial system as well as a method of keeping the "balance" of the family in place. Sharon Wegscheider-Cruse has written about the roles that individual persons learn in disabled families. In her book *Understanding Co-dependency* she identifies five potentially disabling roles played out in families: the enabler, the family hero, the scapegoat, the lost child, and the mascot.

The enabler was probably first identified through the work of AA. What was discovered early on was that when an alcoholic became sober, his or her family often fell apart — the exact opposite of what had been expected. What happened was that the alcoholic's sobriety often caused role confusion in the family, especially for the enabler, who was usually a spouse. The enabler is the person in the family who enabled the alcoholic to continue drinking by providing support. The enablers are conspirators with the alcoholics. They are the ones who made the excuses, earned the living, lied, or in some other ways took much of the discomfort from the alcoholic as he or she progressed in the disease. The enabler either took upon herself or himself the consequences of the alcoholic's behavior or mediated it in such a way that the alcoholic was able to live with the consequences.

The family hero is the person in the family who provides hope and pride. It is important to recall that we are talking about "disabling roles" within the family. There is nothing wrong with providing hope and pride for our families; indeed, we would wish each member to do so. But when it becomes the exclusive job of one member so that that his or her self-worth is tied to that job, rather than God's will, then misery may well be the outcome for that person. Absalom, King David's son, is a good example of the dysfunctional family hero who shakes that role off and eventually turns on his father.

The scapegoat is the family member who gets the blame for the failures and disappointments that the family experiences. In the Old Testament the scapegoat was a sacrificial goat that symbolically carried the sins of the nation. The priest would lay his hands upon the goat, symbolically passing the sins of Israel to the goat, and then it was released into the wilderness where it was eventually killed (cf. Leviticus 16:10). The family scapegoat tends to withdraw from his family and often finds it difficult to commit to community. The scapegoat tends to never feel at home anywhere. Like the scapegoat in Leviticus he or she is put outside the camp.

The lost child is the person in the family who is adept at blending in and adapting. Such individuals accomplish this feat by trying to become invisible and withdrawing from the family's dysfunctional influences. They tend to be loners, bookworms, and dreamers who isolate themselves from others. They are often very lonely and, like the others, have trouble developing healthy and mature relationships.

The mascot tends to be motivated by fear of being left out and forgotten by the family. Mascots want, above all else, to be included and so they will go to great lengths to accomplish that goal. The class clown is a variation on this theme. But the mascot tends to go further than the class clown in that he doesn't mind even being the butt of the joke if that gets him included in the group. Family mascots are hard to ignore, but as a result of their erratic behavior they are rarely taken seriously by their families.

It is worth noting, too, that members of a family may move in and out of these roles. For example, a family hero may become a scapegoat. It is also important to note that we are talking about a problem of degrees. We all play roles. We choose some of the roles, but often they are chosen for us.

Stuart Saves His Family and television's *Married with Children* are rather cynical stories built around the premise of dysfunctional roles. Although these concepts are the stuff of stand-up comedians today like Louis Anderson, we ought not to lose sight of the truth contained in them. We do play roles in our families and in other institutions and organizations, like the parish. We should be conscious and aware of the roles we play in our families of origin and exercise responsible self-criticism concerning these roles.

Family roles can become self-fulfilling prophecies. The classical example is the scapegoat or black sheep of the family. This is the child who is always getting in trouble and always being blamed for the problems in the family. He gets the label and then trouble collects around him like honey attracts flies. The same sort of thing happens when a professional actor becomes typecast. If a woman is cast as a femme fatale over and over again it becomes very difficult for her to break out of that role. Potential roles are ruled out for her even before she has the opportunity to try out for them. This can happen in real life too. It can happen in the family, in the parish, in school, and at work. We need to be attentive and critical of our and other people's roles for just that reason.

Clearly the death of a family member or some other major loss like the loss of a job can be a tremendously destabilizing experience for a disabled family. But once again we can see that grief and loss are opportunities to break through denial and experience a new life. Many studies show the greater the support available in the family after a major loss, the shorter, the more successful, and the more creative is the recovery.

Husbands and Wives, Friends and Lovers

The key trusting relationship is often fulfilled by a spouse. In the case of the death of a spouse, the loss of this confidant relationship is sometimes the most difficult to endure. "If I only had him to talk to about this" is a comment we hear often from those who have lost a loved one. And it just points up how really complex our relationships really are. A husband isn't simply a husband. A wife is not simply a wife. Husbands and wives are confessors, lovers, business partners, counselors, accountants, wage earners, cheerleaders, a parenting team, and on and on, with diverse roles. When a partner is lost, an array of tasks and needful relationships are lost as well. One woman I know said some months after her husband died that she would have to find five or six people to take over the tasks and relationships her husband had filled.

Another real-life problem that affects recovery and reentry is the financial security of the family after a major loss. Families have been stripped of savings and real estate as a result of prolonged illness, death, job loss, or violence. Where strong and resilient extended families exist, they can and do absorb much of the loss of income and wealth. But even in the closest families there are limits. Children grow up and have their own children, retirement, and losses to absorb. So it is important that families make intelligent periodic examinations of their wealth and their ability to absorb major losses. Today, we have available a host of professional financial counselors who can help us make prudent decisions about such things as insurance, savings, stock purchases, health insurance, personal property insurance, and even catastrophic insurance. We often discover that we have more resources than we realized, but we are often sorely unprotected against major losses. Recovery from grief and loss can be made more difficult and painful unless we are prepared to handle the financial problems that are sure to come.

Family Loyalty and New Relationships

Complicating an already complex issue are the other relationships in the family. A man once said of his mother's new husband, "That man can never take my father's place." This was a grown man with his own children referring to the man his mother had married after his father's death.

These feelings are not unusual. People have trouble

learning to care and love the "stranger" who has entered the family because of a sense of being disloyal to the one they have lost. The strong sense of loyalty that families so naturally have can be used to the benefit of the members. It can breed a sense of belonging, intimacy, and security if it is lived out in a healthy way by the parents. But when a parent dies, in the healthiest of families the "new relationship" may well be experienced as threatening and disloyal. Kids from broken homes have an exceedingly difficult time with this, and all the more because Mom or Dad lives just across town, but he or she is never available. This experience can be absolutely tormenting for a child. We strongly identify with what is important to us; with parents, husbands and wives, with careers and dreams, and with places. When we lose a significant part of our life we have to reenter life without the one we cherished. This tends to be a hard road, but it can be made easier by sharing some of the load with another person.

The family is God's creation for the growth and nourishment of children and for the companionship and support it provides for the husband and wife. The family can be a haven where peace and rest can be found. A home in which the members are given the opportunity to grow and test out their wings and a safe harbor when the storms of life rage against them. The Catholic family can be one of the greatest strengths for the person experiencing grief and loss. Of all the resources available to the Catholic, the Church and the family can be the most constant, nurturing, and supportive of all the ways and means available to him or her.

5 Special Problems

Those who have helped Christians through the process of grief recovery for any length of time will encounter special problems that occur often enough to attract special attention. These problems are predictable; indeed, they are rooted in the basic pattern of grief that we have been discussing. But they require special handling. Sometimes, they will require the attention of a professional.

Anniversary and Holiday Grief

A father who had lost his daughter in the Oklahoma disaster said that he and his wife had followed Timothy McVeigh's trial every day. Over time they were able to pick up the pieces and go on with their lives. They resisted it. Getting back into the routine almost made them sick. They were in a regular counseling program in a Christian counseling center in the city. The counseling, their family, and their parish had pulled them through the first, early months of pain. What this father and mother discovered was that when the anniversary of their daughter's death came around, so did all the grief, anger, guilt, and pain. This is anniversary grief. It is not unusual for people to go through the devastating emotions all over again when certain anniversaries come around. Birthdays, wedding anniversaries, anniversaries of the death or funeral all have the power to bring up the emotional reactions again. Just knowing this can be helpful. If we are feeling especially down and we cannot put our finger on the reason, it is worth looking at this as a potential answer.

Closely connected to anniversary grief is holiday grief. Thanksgiving, Christmas, and Easter are often difficult for grieving people. When T. S. Eliot wrote that "April is the cruelest month" in his poem "The Wasteland," some think that he was referring to the contrast between the promise of a new life in the spring and the ever-present reality of death. In a way, that is what many people experience on a very practical level during the holiday season, especially those who have lost loved ones. The festive atmosphere, the joy, the rituals of giving and receiving — all these seem to renew the grief that we thought had been put away. Even very old losses can be recalled with bittersweet memories.

A few years ago a woman who was in a workshop I was conducting in the southern part of the country told me that she simply dreaded Christmas, and she could not bear to hear, much less sing, Christmas hymns and carols. This was her third year without her husband, who had died of cancer. The season of joy for her was a season of poignant memories of what used to be. This is the kind of experience that many people face during the Christmas season, especially those who have suffered recent losses.

The Perfect American Family

One major cause of anxiety and depression during the holidays is the unrealistic expectations many of us live with. One of those unrealistic expectations has to do with the American family. The icons of American family life that most of us grew up with were those *Saturday Evening Post* paintings by Norman Rockwell. Rockwell presents us with images of what could be, maybe what should be. They are all light and sweetness. Rockwell's subjects were drawn from the heartwarming myth of small-town America: the family gathered around the Thanksgiving dinner table, all admiring Grandmother's turkey; the family in church together; a young girl preparing for her first date. Rockwell's paintings stand in contrast to the realities of our families, which are better drawn with a mix of light and shadows.

Another man who took small-town America as his source of inspiration was Sherwood Anderson. His short stories — set in Winesboro, Ohio — present a less idealized vision. His stories focus on people who struggle with isolation and community within the family and within a small American town. Harper Lee's *To Kill a Mockingbird* draws what many of us would consider a more realistic portrait of life in American families. In that novel a single parent does all he can do to raise his children with the grace and courage that his dead wife would have blessed. Harper Lee said that *To Kill a Mockingbird* was a simple love story. It is indeed a love story and a story of a family that mourns well the loss of a mother and a wife. We know that many of our families are broken or breaking. Alcoholism, drug addiction, and even child abuse are not entirely absent from the Church. The real families that we all know and love don't square with Rockwell's vision.

The temptation in a culture where divorce is over fifty percent today is to deny any truth in the Rockwell vision. But that would be incomplete. Maybe he was showing us how it could be rather than how it is. One lesson to learn is that our families don't have to be perfect. Our families may not measure up to Rockwell's image, but with care and attention they can be good, upstanding, and happy Catholic families.

Is It More Blessed to Give Than to Receive?

Another kind of unrealistic expectation during the Christmas season has to do with the ritual of giving and receiving gifts. It is important to set realistic expectations on gift giving, budget, shopping, and time. It is right, even advisable, to sit down with your family and talk truthfully about each other's expectations during the holidays. By doing this you can avoid the letdown and disappointment that will come later on. This is especially true after a major loss such as a death or job loss.

Another way out of the depression is to make a point to be thankful for what we do have and to teach our children the importance of counting their blessings. Remember that a gift of time and of ourselves is much more valuable than a purchased gift. And by all means take time to reflect upon the true meaning of Christmas, which is found in church and not at the mall: "And the Word became flesh and dwelt among us, full of grace and truth; we have beheld his glory, glory as of the only Son from the Father" (John 1:14).

Feast days and seasons are opportunities to renew and strengthen ourselves spiritually.

Including Other People in Our Lives

Loneliness is another contributor to renewed grief during the Christmas or other holiday seasons. Christmas and Thanksgiving often bring back good and bad memories from childhood: parents and loved ones lost, the warmth of close relationships that last and can be counted on. But we and our family members often over-commit ourselves. Shopping, breakfast here, lunch there, dinner somewhere else leave us frazzled. We find ourselves busy, but alone, unconnected because we have not taken the time to be with the people who are most important to us. But we don't have to be alone. We can slow down and spend time with our loved ones.

In addition to those with intact families, there are many people around us who are literally alone. Widows and widowers whose children have moved away are more and more common. And there is an increasing population in our culture who choose not to marry. If we are alone and without family there are still things we can do to escape from isolation. We can invite others to share the holiday with us. Several members of our parish are always on the lookout for single adults and widows who can share Thanksgiving or Christmas with them. We can also go to church and develop a community of support there. Sometimes just calling someone on the phone will brighten up our day as well as that of the person we are calling. We can volunteer with an organization that serves others during Thanksgiving and Christmastime. Sometimes if we concentrate on others rather than ourselves we will find joy. As an old priest used to say, "We do not achieve happiness by pursuing it, but happiness overtakes us when we stop to help another person."

Another cause of holiday grief is stress. We all get frazzled during this time of the year. We try to do too much. Rather than prioritizing, we try to do everything and our holiday calendar fills up. Since we fill our days with activities, we tend to exercise less, and many of us will eat and drink too much. We come away from Thanksgiving or Christmas feeling sluggish and run down. We should watch out for stress and overcommitment.

It is not unusual to be a little down during the holiday seasons. Simple, natural things like getting older or even the weather can trigger sadness. But if the sadness lingers or becomes overwhelming, we should seek professional help. Most of our communities have a fine group of professionals who can help us. If things get to be too much during the holidays, we need to ask for help.

Medical Problems

People sometimes feel shredded by grief. Body, mind, and soul are under unusual stress during the process and so it isn't surprising that medical problems sometimes arise.

Even normal grief can take a heavy physical and emotional toll on us. Sleeplessness, loss of appetite, nervousness, anxiety, fatigue, stomach problems, insomnia, proneness to accidents, dizziness, and even questioning of one's sanity can create wear and tear on the body. This affects our minds and our emotions. Biondi and Puckered, two researchers in Rome, recently published studies suggesting that loss and bereavement make us vulnerable to physical illness and even death during the first two years after the loss. Interestingly, men are a higher risk than women. They also noted that the absence of social support, the unexpectedness of the loss, and concurrent losses could be factors that lead to physical and psychiatric illness.

One obvious potential problem is grief turning into depression. Grief and depression are not the same. Grief is a natural response to a major loss. It is the response to a wound to the whole person. We expect people to be sad when they have suffered a loss. But depression is something else. Depression often arises when one has not properly worked through denial of the reality of the loss and also the feelings that are naturally a part of the loss.

We usually find it difficult to selectively block feelings. If we deny ourselves the feeling of anger, for example, we are likely to end up losing touch with other feelings as well — including such feelings as guilt and sadness and joy. We tend to shut down on the emotional side of things or to make up for the feeling with one we think is more appropriate. Some think that men in our culture tend to block the feeling of sadness and make up for it with anger. And some say that women in our culture do the reverse — they deny anger and make up for the anger with sadness. But the feelings connected with grief are our friends. It is better to enter into the feelings that we are aware of than to have them morphing into other feelings that create a puzzle for us to solve.

Julie, the student whose house burned down, is an example of how unrequited grief can turn into a medical problem. Along with her self-abusive behavior came poor eating habits and lack of sleep that caused her to lose weight and become sick. She also fell into a deep depression. Her depression resulted in uncontrollable weeping, fatigue, and a sense of hopelessness, futility, and even thoughts of suicide. When Julie was able to get in touch with her sadness and anger concerning the loss of her home, she was on the road to recovery.

It is important to recognize depression and get help. Depression doesn't usually cure itself. Most priests today have had extensive training in pastoral counseling and they recognize depression. But most priests are not prepared to offer long-term counseling — nor should they. Yet priests should be aware of counselors in the community to whom they can refer their parishioners. In some parts of the country, dioceses have social-service programs and counselors who are able to help a person through depression or recognize the need for hospitalization.

Self-medication

Grieving people are hurting people. Many of them turn to drugs and alcohol to medicate the pain.

Jenny was one of these people. I met her in a grief-

and-loss group of the psychiatric hospital. Jenny had been admitted to the hospital for alcohol addiction, but it was soon discovered by her social worker that her addiction was complicated by unresolved grief. Jenny was drinking five to seven vodka tonics a night and taking a sedative along with the drinks. She would fall asleep in a drug-induced haze and then awake five or six hours later and get cleaned up for work.

Jenny ran a construction company that specialized in building tennis courts. She had three crews that worked in three states. She and her husband, Sam, had started the very successful business together. He was a heavy-machine operator. One evening as they were shutting down a job, he was driving a bulldozer over a small hill and it turned over on him and crushed him. Jenny and Sam had been having problems. He was drinking too much. They argued frequently. They had an argument the morning he was killed, and she had decided to leave him.

Jenny was devastated by Sam's death. After the funeral she decided to go right back to work in order to stay busy. But she cried all the time. She went to her doctor, who prescribed a sedative to help with her depression. She was hurting even with the drug, so she added the vodka tonics in hopes that she could stop the pain.

Jenny was arrested and put in jail for DWI. That was a blessing, because it helped to break down her denial that she was doing fine and coping with her problems. After she was released from jail she entered a substance-abuse program at the hospital on her own. That saved her life and maybe other lives as well. She was in the program for two weeks and then she entered an outpatient program. Jenny relapsed several times with both the drugs and the alcohol, but within the year she quit both types of substance abuse. She has been sober ever since and has helped several other young women to find sobriety.

Medications are often too easily acquired by grieving people. Doctors, who have received little training in understanding grief, prescribe them too easily, and people supply the medications to friends and relatives almost as though they were passing out chocolates. Jenny was given several tranquilizers by an aunt at Sam's funeral. Medications are sometimes necessary and helpful, but they should only be taken under a doctor's care — and, I must add, from a doctor who knows something about grief. It is important for the caregiver to understand that the point is not to avoid the pain and sadness, but rather to work through it. Jenny was sad and temporarily blocking out her feelings of sadness with a drug that, if it worked, would do her no good. In fact, it did genuine damage to her and it complicated her attempts to complete her grief. She told the group that at the end of the night, even in a medicated and alcoholic haze, she would go to bed crying over Sam.

Attempts at self-medication need to be resisted. Although people attempt self-medication with legal drugs like alcohol, they also abuse prescription medications. Borrowing medications from friends and relatives can lead to obvious difficulties. It is illegal for one thing. Unless we are physicians trained in drug therapy we could construct for ourselves and others a maze of addictions and complications that will make bereavement all the more difficult, if not impossible.

Complicated Grief

Grief sometimes goes wrong. Dr. Teresa A. Rando, a noted grief therapist and researcher, recognizes seven circumstances that could complicate mourning: (1) infant death, (2) unexpected death, (3) preventable deaths like suicide, (4) terminal illness and the stress that ensues from the financial and emotional demands of extended care, (5) inappropriately dependent or ambivalent relationship between the mourner and deceased, (6) absence of social support, and (7) emotional and mental illness such as depression and anxiety.

When mourning doesn't go as it should — through the proper stages on to resolution and reentry into life — we should pay close attention. People can get stuck anywhere in the process, and that can lead to serious mental and physical illness. Jenny is a case in point. The issues that complicated her grief were her dependence on alcohol and the sedative she was taking, her troubled marriage and the looming separation, the unexpected death of her husband, the accidental nature of the death, and her developing depression. It is easy to see how these issues, added to an already stressful and sad occasion, could interfere with the grieving process.

Four complications to grief are worth looking at briefly: (1) when grieving doesn't start, (2) when it doesn't end, (3) when it becomes exaggerated, and (4) when it is masked grief. These are potentially very serious, even life-threatening problems, and we need to know how to look for professional help. The parish priest is our first line of defense. He has been well-trained by his seminary and he knows the importance of finding good professional help. Usually, the pastor knows at least some of the mental health professionals in the community and so he is the person to start with in seeking a specialist. One approach to avoid is trying to find a counselor through the yellow pages of the phone book. If your pastor doesn't know immediately whom to refer you to, he will be able to find out.

When We Can't Start Grieving

Sometimes it appears that grieving doesn't begin well in some people. J. William Worden calls this delayed grief, and he makes the point that in some way the emotional response to the loss is significantly below what would normally be expected. For some reason the person has suppressed the grief reaction. "The person may experience some emotions, but it (the emotion reaction) is not sufficient to the loss. At a future date the person may experience the symptoms of grief over some subsequent and immediate loss, but the intensity of his or her grieving seems excessive. What is happening here is that some of the grieving . . . which was not adequately done at the time of the original loss, is carried forward and is being experienced at the time of the current loss. The person generally has the distinct impression that the response [he or she is] experiencing is exaggerated vis-à-vis the current situation" (Grief Counseling and Grief Therapy).

The way we can identify "delayed grief" is in the inhibited grief reaction to the original loss and excessiveness of a current loss. We can see exactly that kind of reaction in Julie, the college student whose childhood home burned down. Her emotional reactions at the time of the loss were not permitted to come to full bloom because she was in school, and her parents didn't want her to come home and miss out on her classes. She spiraled downward over the next year, at times experiencing intense emotions of sadness, guilt, and anger, but without referring those feelings back to the original loss of her home. She knew something was wrong and that her reactions were inappropriate to the present context, but it wasn't until she sought professional help that she was able to identify the central grief. When she was put in touch with the original loss and its great significance for her, she was able to enter into the original pain that had been delayed. With the help of her peers in group therapy she was able to make genuine strides toward health.

When We Can't Stop Grieving

There are also occasions when it appears that grieving doesn't come to an end with the person reentering life. Grieving people get stuck in the process and seem to be unable to extricate themselves from it. Worden calls this chronic grief. It is, as he puts it, "excessive in duration, and never comes to a satisfactory conclusion . . . (and) the person undergoing the reaction is very much aware that he or she is not getting through the period of mourning. . . . People coming for help will say things like, 'I'm not getting back to living,' 'This thing is not ending for me,' 'I need help to be myself again' " (*Grief Counseling and Grief Therapy*).

This is fairly easy to recognize in ourselves and others, if we are not faking our real feelings. In most cases it is clear that the person is stuck. Jenny, whose husband had died in the bulldozer accident, was suffering from chronic grief. Her drug addiction interfered with her grieving, and thus she continued on for months attempting to medicate her pain. She was not successful. And full, vigorous reentry into life continued to elude her. It was only when she took time out from her medicated routine by entering the hospital that she came to grips with her issues.

It is best with chronic grief, as well as with all complicated grief experiences, that we seek professional help.

Am I Overreacting?

Third, Worden refers to exaggerated grief reactions. The feelings of fear, anger, sadness, and guilt can become so exaggerated that they develop into full-blown depression, phobias, and despair. People who are experiencing an exaggerated grief reaction are usually aware of their reaction and its relationship to the loss — and the depression, despair, or phobias have become disabling. It is clearly a normal part of grief to experience fearful thoughts and feelings. But if these feelings become so exaggerated as to become disabling, then a complicated grief reaction has developed. One person after the loss of her father became so fearful of death that she was unable to leave her house for long periods of time. She was unable to take vacations or hold down a job. Family intervention was necessary to break through the problems. How do we recognize an exaggerated reaction? All of the emotions we have pointed to here are normal for a bereaved person. However, time seems to be one of the best benchmarks. It is not unusual to feel blown away and disabled by a loss. We may well experience despair, fear, and depression. "I can't live without her" is a common reaction to the death of a loved one. It isn't especially alarming to hear this sort of comment at first, but if the disposition continues over a matter of weeks, then a problem probably exists and one should seek professional help.

What Am I Hiding?

Finally, Worden refers to masked grief reaction. As he puts it, "Patients experience symptoms and behaviors which cause them difficulty but do not see or recognize the fact that these are related to the loss." Masked grief may manifest itself in a physical symptom or in inappropriate behavior and the same sort of feelings that would be manifested in an exaggerated grief reaction. The difference between the two is that in the exaggerated grief the person is aware of the experience and its link to his or her loss. That awareness is missing in masked grief. The person doesn't see the relationship between his or her symptoms and the loss. People suffering the loss of a loved one don't experience themselves as grieving the loss. Some researchers have speculated that this unmanifested grief occurs within individuals whose egos are not sufficiently developed to cope with the stress of the grief work. Worden cites Helen Deutch, a clinical researcher, who stated that masked grief will eventually become overt and fully expressed in some other way. This usually happens in two ways: The grief may be disguised in some physical symptom or it may manifest itself in aberrant behavior. Pain is a common psychosomatic complaint of masked grief. On the other hand, inappropriate behavior — such as drug or alcohol abuse or some other form of acting out — may also be manifestations of unowned, or unacknowledged, grief.

All four of these complications are experienced in degrees by everyone. We may well ask such questions as: "At what point does ordinary denial become the 'can't start grieving' complication?" "How is 'I can't stop grieving' recognized?" "How long does normal grief take?" Again, time will tell. One of the major issues for normal grieving and complicated grieving is that a person experiencing normal grief can do reality testing. That becomes nearly impossible for most people who experience complicated grief. Look at these symptoms as red flags. When you see a red flag, slow down and take another look. Become more attentive. Be intelligent. It is important at this stage to begin consultation with a mental health professional.

Helping Bereaved Children to Mourn

Contrary to popular myth, children do grieve and they present us with a special set of problems. They mourn like children and not like adults, so they need help in processing the loss and their own feelings. They have experienced few losses in their lives that they are aware of, so there is little or no reference point for them. They also have fewer coping skills than adults, and their little egos are still undergoing formation. This is especially true with children between the ages of five and seven. Anniversary grief may be especially intense for children as they grow up into adulthood. There are some practical steps that we can take with our children in order to prepare them for loss. Worden points out that "mourning for a childhood loss can be revived at many points in an adult's life when it is reactivated during important life events." Baptisms, confirmations, marriages, and funerals are capable of bringing up this grief.

With little children we can take what is a typical experience for a child — the death of a pet — and use it as an opportunity to teach the child about death. There's nothing sacrilegious about putting together a little funeral with prayers. This provides the child with an opportunity to do something for the pet. It also gives the parent an opportunity to talk with the child about death and loss from a specifically Christian point of view.

Older children can often be helped by sensitively applying some principles of grieving that work for adults.

Chad was an eleven-year-old boy who became deeply depressed after his older brother was killed in a skateboarding accident. He was placed in a grief-and-loss group with the other children, and after a few days of building trust he was willing to talk about his brother. He had had an argument with his brother on the way home that day; they had exchanged angry words, and Chad left his brother alone. By the time Chad arrived home his mom was rushing out the driveway on the way to the hospital. His brother had been hit by a car while crossing the street. His brother died within hours.

At the funeral Chad was already feeling deep guilt over his brother's death. He felt that somehow the argument had caused his death. In addition, the brothers couldn't make up now that he was gone. The group suggested that Chad write a letter to his brother and say everything to him in the letter that he needed to say. It was suggested that he talk about his feelings of guilt, anger, and sadness. At the next session he came to the group with a smile on his face, and the group knew that the work was well under way. He read the letter he had written to his dead brother. He apologized for the argument and his angry words. He asked for forgiveness and spoke about how much he loved his brother and how much he missed him. That was a breakthrough for the young man and shortly after he returned home.

Some Do's and Don'ts

Children are often the forgotten mourners. Well-meaning friends and relatives often try to protect the child from the experience of loss. Depending on the age of the child, he or she will have predictable responses to a loss. An infant, for example, has no understanding of death, but he or she does experience separation and, as any mother knows, is tuned in to the parents' emotions in an uncanny way. Help the child identify and express his or her feeling over the loss. Young children of pre-school age have a hard time grasping the permanency of death or any other loss for that matter. Toddlers up to about six years old may view death as something like sleeping; but they may also understand it as violent punishment, caused by anger, and even something that is "catching" that will get them. A little child of this age group sees himself as the center of the universe. For example, he may therefore think that his anger toward a person caused his or her death. From the age of five to about eleven or twelve, children will come to have a more realistic understanding of the irreversibility, and even the inevitability, of death. But at first they view it as something that only happens to other people. Death doesn't seem possible for them. Once children move into the teenage years they develop an adult understanding of death.

When explaining death to children, canned answers should be avoided. Don't tell them, for instance, that

Mom or Dad has "gone to sleep," "is resting," "has been taken by God," or other phrases that will communicate something to the child that we do not intend. In the child's literal, concrete world this will only be confusing. Don't tell children that the person died because of sickness. Everyone gets sick, including children, and it is wise not to set up problems for the future. Instead we should explain that "Mom or Dad was very sick. He was so sick that his body stopped working." Don't relate death to the medical community and practice: the hospital, the nurses, the surgeon, or the surgery. As we have already pointed out, attributing the death to God's action should be avoided. Regardless of how you understand that theologically, it will only confuse the child and present him with an image of God that is unbiblical: "God took Mommy or Daddy to heaven because he or she was such a good person." It isn't unknown in the annals of child psychology for a child to react to a thought with bad behavior in order to avoid death and to develop an unbiblical fear of God. Your priest can help here. And remember, never lie to children. But there is much that we should and can do to help our children understand and grieve over loss.

Even before a major loss, like the death of a family member or a close friend, we can encourage our children to ask questions about death. For example, when pets die we can use that as a teaching opportunity to discuss death on the children's level. In passages like the Sermon on the Mount where Jesus all but says that God attends the funeral of little birds, we have an opportunity to instill a Catholic understanding of death and God's loving, steadfast character in the child. It is appropriate to have a little funeral for the pet and read Scripture and let the child talk about his or her relationship to the animal. This way we can help the young person develop the practice of prayer and ritual. Funerals for pets will help children become somewhat familiar with what is certainly to be a bewildering experience when they experience the death of a family member or a close friend.

When children experience grief, they often act out in pronounced ways. Depending on their age, they may regress somewhat, returning to thumb-sucking, fear of the dark, bed-wetting, baby talk, and crying. Bedtime can become a difficult experience for children who are fearful of separation from their parents or caregivers. The older the children, the closer their behavior will be to that of adults, as they experience grief and loss: guilt, fear, anxiety, separation anxiety, headaches and abdominal pain, hostility, short attention, withdrawal, and poor grades; in some cases there are children who even manifest similar symptoms of the deceased person. All of these are red flags for the parents.

Red flags mean that we need to attend to grieving children and give them opportunities to deal with their loss. Most children need to talk about the loss a lot. Like adults they can tells stories over and over again, seemingly never tiring of them. Art, finger painting, and storytelling may help children in expressing their feelings. Youngsters are capable of expressing real feelings of sadness and fear. They love photographs. Looking through a family album with Mom and Dad can be a way to encourage the child to talk about his or her feelings and to tell stories that help the young person. Some people encourage children to write a letter to express their grief.

Remember to reassure the child of his or her own safety. Don't use distractions to "protect" the child. Also remember that children in mourning need to know what to expect in the future. They need to be assured that they will be taken care of and how. They need to know that family and friends will be sad and grieving. A lot of people will be coming by the house. If it is appropriate, the grieving children should be told what will happen at the funeral and even given an opportunity to help out appropriately. Help them see the funeral as a time for saying good-bye to the loved one. At the same time it is good to include your priest to help the children understand what Catholics believe concerning heaven and everlasting life. Don't force grief-stricken youngsters to go to the funeral if they resist it strongly, but keep the door open.

It is OK for kids to cry, but sometimes they need permission and even modeling. At the same time they need to know that it is fine if they don't cry, if that is the way particular children usually handle loss. It is very important that you listen to grieving children. Physical touch as well as affirming your love for them is important at this time. For a while their lives will seem upside down and it will take a little time for the family to get back into a routine.

If the child is old enough to love, he or she is old enough to mourn. If we pay attention to the children and not try to be too overprotective they will usually tell us what they need to do and to know. They can help us understand how they mourn. We have to begin by listening to them and not hiding the loss from them.

6 Christian Forgiveness

The pain and miseries of grief lead us, as the *Book of Common Prayer* tells us, directly to the mysteries of grace: "In the midst of life we are in death; of whom may we seek for succor, but of thee, O Lord, who for our sins art justly displeased?" The process of coming to terms with people and places and parts of our lives that are irrevocably gone, and then reentering our lives in a new way, brings us to the heart of what God did for us in Jesus Christ. In the midst of our loss, we find God.

As Catholics, we experience this in the glorious richness of the Church. The first of these mysteries is that of forgiveness. Whenever our Lord healed, he forgave. And forgiveness from his perspective was not simply a way to endure our broken lives, but it was rather an end in itself. It was an end in itself because it is the embodiment of healing. The wounds of the past, self-inflicted or inflicted by other people, can be healed. The converse is also true: Since we have sinned against other people, we can become instruments of healing. In the midst of our loss, we often come face to face with sin. We discover that we have held grudges, that we have enemies, that we have inflicted pain. We have been sinned against and we have sinned against other people. The Catholic answer to this very human condition is Christian forgiveness.

Then Peter approaching asked him, "Lord, if my brother sins against me, how often must I forgive him? As many as seven times?" Jesus answered, "I say to you, not seven times but seventy-seven times. That is why the kingdom of heaven may be likened to a king who decided to settle accounts with his servants. When he began the accounting, a debtor was brought before him who owed him a huge amount. Since he had no way of paying it back, his master ordered him to be sold, along with his wife, his children, and all his property, in payment of the debt. At that, the servant fell down, did him homage, and said, 'Be patient with me, and I will pay you back in full.' Moved with compassion the master of that servant let him go and forgave him the loan. When that servant had left, he found one of his fellow servants who owed him a much smaller amount. He seized him and started to choke him, demanding, 'Pay back what you owe.' Falling to his knees, his fellow servant begged him, 'Be patient with me, and I will pay you back.' But he refused. Instead he had him put in prison until he paid back the debt. Now when his fellow servants saw what had happened, they were deeply disturbed, and went to their master and reported the whole affair. His master summoned him and said to him, 'You wicked servant! I forgave you your entire debt because you begged me to. Should you not have had pity on your fellow servant, as I had pity on you?'

Then in anger his master handed him over to the torturers until he should pay the whole debt. So will my heavenly Father do to you, unless each of you forgives his brother from his heart.

— *MATTHEW 18:21-35 (NAB)*

Forgiveness Is Not Therapy

In the movie *Mission*, Robert De Niro plays a man who makes a living capturing native Indians who live in the jungles of Brazil. He sells them as slaves. Those he cannot capture he kills. At the beginning of the film, he kills his own brother in a fit of rage and then he falls into deep remorse. Months later a priest comes to him, shows concern and compassion, and hears his confession. Upon leaving he gives him a penance, an outward and visible way of showing remorse. A burden of objects — his sword, shield, and other instruments of his former violent life — are tied up in a net and then attached to his back with a long, thick rope. Everywhere he goes, he must drag this heavy burden as his penance.

He follows the missionaries back into the jungle to the very tribe he had formerly exploited. The Indians had only recently been evangelized by one of the missionaries, played by Jeremy Irons. In one scene De Niro climbs an extraordinarily steep cliff with his heavy burden dangling behind him. Its weight is so great and clumsy that we almost expect him to fall to his death on the rocks below. When he reaches the top of the cliff, waiting for him are the very Indians he had ravaged and murdered. One of the young warriors draws a sharp knife and places it at De Niro's throat. Then the Indian, to the relief of everyone, takes the rope in hand and cuts his former enemy free of his burden. We watch his burden fall to the water below.

This powerful image dramatically depicts the radical nature of forgiveness — Christian forgiveness: "Forgive us our sins, as we forgive those who have sinned against us" (cf. Matthew 6:12 and Luke 11:4).

This kind of forgiveness does not come naturally. In a state of nature we tend to seek and destroy that which would destroy us or ours. If we are stuck with only that which we inherit from nature, then we follow the rules: "Might makes right." "An eye for an eye." "Revenge." Or the contemporary American corporate axiom: "Don't get mad, get even."

But if our baptism into the Body of Christ means anything, it means that we are not at the mercy of nature. We have been born again through the sacrament of baptism and we are thus called upon, with the aid of the Holy Spirit and the Blessed Sacrament and indeed the whole Catholic community, to nurture our new life — to nurture our new nature. St. Paul says as much when he writes to the Romans: "Do you not know that all of us who have been baptized into Christ Jesus were baptized into his death? We were buried therefore with him by baptism into death, so that as Christ was raised from the dead by the glory of the Father, we too might walk in newness of life" (6:3-4).

In our baptismal promise we (through our sponsors) renounce sin by way of renouncing the world, the flesh, and the devil. The notion of the "sinful desires of the flesh" sounds strange to our ears today. In our day and time if people even mention the "sinful desires of the flesh" in a conversation it's usually to lighten things up and make a joke. No one talks that way anymore. The notion of taking "sinful desires of the flesh" seriously, most would say, is out of the Middle Ages and smacks of self-hatred. Somehow "psychiatric issues" are more believable.

This is one of the things that make forgiveness so difficult in our culture. We have become so psychologically oriented. Guilt is thought of in terms of feelings and psychological states more than in terms of a condition or a relationship. When we listen to people it seems that "feelings of guilt" are real, but the notion of really being *guilty* is not. "If I can just feel better, less guilty, then I'll be all right." A host of television talk show personalities and experts seem to be telling us that we have every right to hold on to our grudges. This kind of thinking even influences the twelve-step movement. There are those who would suggest that if we get into recovery and get into the right twelve-step program we don't have to bother with the hard work of forgiveness. Christians occasionally come away from the twelve-step experience with the impression that they have the right to hold a grudge, while instinctively knowing that as Christians that is not true.

The truth is that we have all sinned against our brothers and sisters in Christ. And we have all been sinned against. People have had real damage done to them by other people. We have to strike a balance in our lives to recognize these realities. Not affirming them is to sin against the victim once again, but to make "being sinned against" the entire focus is to perpetuate a culture of victimhood within the Church. We must be careful not to blame victims, and at the same time we must be careful not to encourage self-pity, holding grudges, and unchristian behavior in the name of having been victimized.

The Christian ideal of forgiveness is the answer. The Church calls upon us to recognize the harm that sin has done in our lives and in the lives of others; but in light of the death of Christ on our behalf, she seeks to grant clemency. The obligation to forgive is placed squarely upon our shoulders:

> Our Father who art in heaven,
> Hallowed be thy name.

Thy kingdom come,
Thy will be done,
 On earth as it is in heaven.
Give us this day our daily bread;
And forgive us our debts,
 As we also have forgiven our debtors;
And lead us not into temptation,
 But deliver us from evil.
For if you forgive men their trespasses, your
heavenly Father also will forgive you; but if you do
not forgive men their trespasses, neither will your
Father forgive your trespasses.

— *MATTHEW 6:9-15*

In 1981, a Turkish terrorist by the name of Mehmet Ali Agca positioned himself in a joyous crowd of well-wishers as Pope John Paul passed by in his motorcade. When the Holy Father's car came slowly by the crowd, the terrorist pulled a gun from his pocket and shot John Paul, seriously wounding him. Had the police not intervened, the crowd might have killed the would-be assassin. John Paul was rushed to the hospital and his life was saved. When he was released, the Pope paid a visit to Mehmet Ali Agca in the jail. There before the watching world, he followed in the footsteps of our Lord as he forgave the man who would have killed him. The Holy Father incarnated mercy for the whole world to see.

It is important to remember that this piece of the Christian life isn't just for popes and the super-holy. It is the work of the whole people of God. Forgiving a person who has harmed us may well be one of the most difficult achievements of our lives. We have to resist the tendency today to redefine this Christian duty into a therapeutic exercise. We have to be careful not to replace sin with "issues" and "addictions."

While "recovery" cannot take the place of salvation

and sanctification, there are certainly therapeutic benefits to forgiving someone who has harmed you. It is remarkable how often forgiveness comes up for the spiritually and emotionally broken among us. It is a critical point of growth for members of AA to do a fearless inventory of the harm they have done to other people and also to be willing to make amends where possible. When marriage counseling is successful, it always ends in a recognition of how the husband and wife have sinned against each other and how forgiveness and reconciliation are provided for them through the Church. An astonishing number of "psychiatric cases" would evaporate if the sacrament of penance were applied on the one hand, and if Christian forgiveness were extended on the other.

But forgiveness from a Christian point of view is not merely a therapeutic exercise by which we let go of a painful experience. Neither is it a form of "conflict resolution," where people get together and arrive at a win-win solution to conflict. Forgiveness is a spiritual discipline. It takes volition, persistence, and practice to forgive someone who has really harmed you.

In a way, forgiveness is like acquiring a taste for something exotic. At first it seems undesirable and we wonder why anyone would want it. But it grows on us. We develop the taste. In the case of forgiveness, to develop the taste is to be changed more into the likeness of Christ. The theologian L. Gregory Jones compares forgiveness to a craft — a craft that we cannot do without God's help. God's help comes through his Church, through the community of faithful Christians — or perhaps I should say people trying to be faithful Christians. We cannot do it alone. The good news is that we do not have to do it alone. We have the Church. We have the Word of God. We have the sacraments. We have the encouragement as well as the accountability that comes only through the Church in parish life.

Spiritual progress in our own lives is marked by our willingness to extend forgiveness to those who have harmed us: to enemies, to those who mistreat us, to those who spitefully use us. Christian love is made very real through forgiveness. To forgive those who have wounded us is to grow into the moral and spiritual likeness of God. "Be merciful even as your Father is merciful" (cf. Mark 11:25).

Spiritual progress in the Christian life does not happen without forgiveness. In *Lord, Teach Us*, their book on the Lord's Prayer, theologians William H. Willimon and Stanley Hauerwas make a salient point: "Can we agree that forgiveness is an outrageous human act? In our society where might makes right, a society of a myriad of victims, each licking his or her cherished wounds, forgiveness seems crazy. Furthermore, there are many misunderstandings of what Christians mean when we speak of forgiveness.

"So right here is where the Lord's Prayer is most difficult to pray. Perhaps that is why this is the longest and most involved petition in the Lord's Prayer. As usual, it first asks God to do something for us. Then it promises that we will do something for others. Before there is any talk in the prayer about forgiving anyone else, we are made to ask for forgiveness ourselves. Before there is any consideration of the wrongs that we have suffered, we are made to ponder the great wrong God has suffered through us."

The point that we have been seeing over and over again is that our losses open up spiritual opportunities. Forgiveness — our own forgiveness and our extension of forgiveness to others — is one of the most powerful opportunities in our lives. Forgiveness is at the center of the life of Christ. In his teaching in the Lord's Prayer Jesus places it at the center of the life of the Church and our lives individually.

The Communion of Saints

How does a grieving person deal with the issue of forgiveness when the person to forgive or to seek forgiveness from is dead? How can reconciliation happen if the person is not here to be reconciled?

Catholics believe that the departed person is not really gone. The deceased is still part of the communion of saints. This New Testament teaching is a doctrine of comfort. The communion of saints is about our mutual incorporation into the Body of Christ; it is not about communication between the Church militant and the Church triumphant. As we have already seen, the Bible and the Church flatly deny us the opportunity to communicate with the departed. What the apostolic writers and the Church promise is that we are all "in Christ," and therefore we share a real, lively fellowship with the whole Church — living and departed. The departed do not cease to be members of the Body of Christ.

The communion of saints is understood, in both the Eastern and Western Church, as a fellowship of mutual intercessory prayer. In the Eastern Church this doctrine is a living reality that extends to all of those who have died in the Lord. No distinctions are made between the "saints" and other departed Christians. The Eastern Church tends to view the communion of saints as an august, joyous, and approachable throng who worship around the throne of God. For example, prayers may be offered up for the "saints" on the one hand, while on the other hand, prayers may be requested from friends who have recently died in the Lord. The Western Church leans toward a similar understanding of those departed in our Lord. We pray for them and they pray for us. Our fellowship is in the Lord, however, and not in communication between one another. Thus as we draw near to Jesus, we draw near to the blessed departed.

In that context we may offer up our forgiveness for

wrongs done to us, and we may offer up broken and contrite hearts to our Lord over the sins we have committed against the departed. If we are surrounded by a great cloud of witnesses, as the writer of Hebrews says (12:1), then it seems reasonable that our offering will be taken up into the consciousness of the whole Body of Christ. Our fellowship within the communion of saints is within the experience of prayer and worship, especially in the Eucharist, as we look forward to the day of full consummation when we will be with loved ones and former enemies. And Jesus will wipe away all our tears and death will be no more.

7 Dealing with Anger

Anger is a frequent visitor in the household of the grieving. Quite often, this visitor will settle down for an extended stay — an uninvited long-term guest. People in mourning often experience anger at God, asking such questions as, "Why did God take my loved one?" "Why doesn't he heal this sickness?" "Why has this situation turned out so badly?" We can be angry at ourselves. And we can struggle with feelings of anger at someone who is dead. Anger, in short, is a major problem.

It is important for us to remember that anger is an emotion, and emotions are neither good nor bad. They simply exist. What we do with the feelings is another issue. Feelings tell us something. But acting out feelings can be physically, emotionally, and spiritually destructive. Anger, for example, may communicate our feelings about being treated unjustly. If I am singled out by my employer and treated unfairly because I remind her of someone she dislikes, it would be unnatural for me not to feel anger about that issue. The same may well be the case within a marriage, a parish, or a community. Emotions communicate. But acting out destructive feelings will not lead to maturity nor is it likely to lead to resolving the problem according to Christian principles.

All emotions color our perception of reality. The emotion of anger is right up there with romantic love in its ability to distort our grasp of reality. Love is not blind. Rather, love sees beauty, grace, courage, and character when others cannot see such attributes in an individual. Anger, on the other hand, is often blind. Where beauty, grace, courage, and character do exist in a person who has sinned against us, our anger may well blind us to those higher qualities in the person. When that occurs we are caught in the process of self-justification. We can make no spiritual progress this way.

Anger happens. Thus, it is critically important to have someone we trust to help us work through our anger. A priest or a spiritual director would be especially appropriate for this task. We need a trusted friend who can help us when we cannot see the forest for the trees. We need someone who knows enough about us emotionally and spiritually to give us mature advice on how and when to take action. Someone with whom we feel safe can help us do reality testing.

Anger is an issue in two places — in relationships with one another in the Body of Christ and in our relationship with God himself. We will look at both — starting with our anger with other people.

Admission

It may be surprising to many Christians and non-Christians that St. Paul gives a positive place to anger in the Body of Christ. He not only acknowledges the reality of the experience in the following passage quoted from Ephesians, but he goes on to give specific directions on how to process the feeling between people within the

Christian community: "Therefore, putting away false-hood, let every one speak the truth with his neighbor, for we are members one of another. Be angry but do not sin; do not let the sun go down on your anger, and give no opportunity to the devil. . . . Let all bitterness and wrath and anger and clamor and slander be put away from you, with all malice, and be kind to one another, tenderhearted, forgiving one another, as God in Christ forgave you" (Ephesians 4:25-27; 31-32).

Several things have to happen for us to process anger appropriately between one another. First, we need to be honest about being angry. It does us no good at all to keep the denial going. Of course, denial is a strong delusion. We usually are unaware of it ourselves. Those close to us can help us see it.

One of the dangers of denying anger is that we tend to project our repressed and unowned (that is, unac-knowledged) feelings onto someone else. Brice Avery, a psychiatrist who lives in Scotland and who has published widely in pastoral care, explains projection this way: "Pro-jection . . . is driven by anxiety and leads to denial of the way we really feel. Subsequently we split off those feel-ings from our conscious selves and deposit them on to someone else whom we then despise. The things we dis-like the most in others are the things we hate in our-selves but won't face up to. The proof of this last step is that other people respond to the projection; they identify with it. This is called projective identification. . . . I mis-take someone else's emotional projections onto me for my own feelings. If I don't know what's going on I am likely to act upon the projective identification. Even if I repress my desire to act upon the feelings I am still con-taining the other person's aggression for him: someone will catch it later" (*The Pastoral Encounter*).

A man in my parish once told me that he was never angry with anyone. He was actually quite angry about a number of things in his life, but he thought that he had to pretend that he wasn't in order to have the respect of the parish. He thought it was unspiritual to be angry. In truth, it was unspiritual to deny what was really the case in his life.

My friend actually projected his anger onto his wife. She carried his anger for him. He couldn't get angry, but she could. Everyone liked him because he was always nice. No one could stand being around her because she was always angry. She had accepted her husband's projection of her as an angry person — that is, she had responded to her husband's projection and identified with it. That is neither spiritual nor honest.

One of our first duties in the Church is not allowing ourselves or others to lie. This is not as easy as it sounds. It requires trust, honesty, and a loving attitude toward one another. Truth and mercy go together. Truth without mercy is like the letter of the law that kills. Mercy without truth is little more than permissiveness. The balance is learning to "speak the truth in love" first to ourselves and then to others. Thus, in dealing with our anger, the first task is admitting the actual anger we have. Again, I cannot stress too much the importance of having a priest or spiritual director to walk with us through our anger.

Identification

The first step is to admit the anger. The second step is to determine the exact nature of the behavior that has caused our anger. As we are told in the New Testament: "If your brother sins against you, go and tell him his fault, between you and him alone. If he listens to you, you have gained your brother. But if he does not listen, take one or two others along with you, that every word may be confirmed by the evidence of two or three witnesses. If he refuses to listen to them, tell it to the church;

and if he refuses to listen even to the church, let him be to you as a Gentile and a tax collector" (Matthew 18:15-17).

Our Lord said about relationships within the Church, "If your brother does something wrong . . . " (cf. Matthew 18:15), we must know the exact nature of that wrong. Free-floating anger has to be identified. What is the issue? Why are we angry? How have we been offended or harmed by this person? For example, if the person has called us a name or slandered us in some way, then that is probably the cause of our anger. That is a real harm. It only takes a moment of reflection upon the stories we have told to realize the objects of our potential anger. We become angry at parents, siblings, spouses, children, priests, doctors, close friends, and even God. The second issue for us, though, is to determine the exact nature of the behavior that has angered us.

Loving, Honest Confrontation

The third step is the most difficult. It requires going to the person who has angered us by his or her behavior and telling the person about it. St. Paul puts this in unmistakable terms for the Christian: "Therefore, putting away falsehood, let every one speak the truth with his neighbor, for we are members one of another. Be angry but do not sin; do not let the sun go down on your anger, and give no opportunity to the devil" (Ephesians 4:25-27).

Again, Jesus' instructions are to the point and astonishingly direct: "If your brother sins against you, go and tell him his fault, between you and him alone. If he listens to you, you have gained your brother" (Matthew 18:15).

This calls for maturity — or at least a willingness to grow into maturity. We should take this step only after we have prayed and reflected over it for a period of time. Then before the actual confrontation we should share the issues surrounding this step with a trusted counselor like a priest or spiritual director. This is a delicate step that requires humility and resolve. We should be in a relationship with a spiritual director, a priest, or some other person competent to deal with these issues, someone we can trust to help us discern the appropriate time and manner of the confrontation. Ultimately, whether or not the offending person responds to us favorably, we must maintain an attitude of love. Remember the truth about forgiveness: Before we confront our brother or sister, we go to God first and ask for forgiveness for all the wrongs we have done him. We can in no way lord it over the other person, even if we are rebuffed, as occasionally will be the case.

This kind of healing is possible only if we acknowledge the reality of our anger and with God's help attempt to bring something healing and redemptive out of it. We do not have God's permission to nurse our anger into resentment, bitterness, and destructive behavior. Remember that feelings are neutral, but destructive behavior is not. Destructive behavior is unacceptable in our lives as Catholics. Angry behavior is the spiritual undoing of ourselves as well as of the person we may be angry with.

One of the best ways to deal with our own feelings of anger toward another person is to pray for that person in a spirit of humility. I think most of us would find it very difficult, if not impossible, to nurse a grudge toward a person if we are genuinely praying for him or her. And it is important to remember that we are praying for the person in a spirit of humility, recalling the words of Jesus that "we must forgive from the bottom of our hearts" those who have sinned against us if we want to be forgiven ourselves. Most of us have plenty of sin, failure, and wasted opportunities in our own lives to regret without becoming cynically attached to those who have sinned against us. As we practice this spiritual discipline of praying for our enemy we will be using our own anger as a motivation to spiritual growth. We will be working with God to bring good out of evil.

Morton Kelsey has written with insight about the steps we Christians must take to love our enemies: "That step consists of ceasing to do anything unkind to the enemy. This is so obvious that it should not even be necessary to suggest it. As long as we express our anger or hostility in punitive action, in reprisal or in any form of attack, financial, physical or psychological, there is no hope that our 'love-liking' toward that person will increase. These actions wear deeper the rut of our anger so that the wheels of our lives are less able to get out of the groove of hostility. Acts of retribution feed the fire of hatred" (*Caring: How Can We Love One Another?*).

A writer associated with Alcoholics Anonymous has this reflection on anger that applies well beyond the bounds of twelve-step programs: "Even if we actually have been treated shabbily or unjustly, resentment is a luxury that, as alcoholics, we cannot afford. For us, all anger is self-destructive, because it can lead us back to drinking."

Lance Webb in his book *Conquering the Seven Deadly Sins* describes a painting by Peter Brueghel — done in 1558 and entitled "Wrath" — that illustrates the destructive nature of anger: "Wrath is pictured with a knife in his mouth, a vial of poison in one hand and the other hand in a sling, having been injured in previous battle, and sitting astride a barrel filled with fighting and dying men. Behind Wrath is a warrior's tent where a naked human body is being turned on a spit over the fire and a long-nosed helper is pouring a ladle of burning lead over the body, while the vultures outside pick the bones of other victims. In the foreground and background of the painting are processions of warriors in armor, with all kinds of murderous implements, trampling on their victims. Around the angry killers, rise the flames of destruction."

The truth is that none of us can afford the acerbic and potentially spirit-destroying consequences of unattended anger. Within the Church we are indeed blessed with the gift of the Blessed Sacrament and the sacrament of penance in which we can directly address these feelings and with the help of a priest, a spiritual director, or simply a wise and trusted spiritual friend, we make a constructive end to it.

Anger with God

"The same night he arose and took his two wives, his two maids, and his eleven children, and crossed the ford of the Jabbok. He took them and sent them across the stream, and likewise everything that he had. And Jacob was left alone; and a man wrestled with him until the breaking of the day. When the man saw that he did not prevail against Jacob, he touched the hollow of his thigh; and Jacob's thigh was put out of joint as he wrestled with him. Then he said, 'Let me go, for the day is breaking.' But Jacob said, 'I will not let you go, unless you bless me.' And he said to him, 'What is your name? And he said, 'Jacob.' Then he said, 'Your name shall no more be called Jacob, but Israel, for you have striven with God and with men, and have prevailed' " (Genesis 32:22-28).

Though this passage from Genesis concerning Jacob's wrestling with God does not speak directly to anger toward God, it nonetheless speaks to the cure. The answer is the same as the advice of Matthew 18. Just as we are to go to a brother or sister whom we feel has treated us unjustly, so we ought to go to God as well.

In his film, *The Apostle*, Robert Duvall presents one scene that beautifully expresses this. The preacher — played by Duvall — after a heartbreaking experience with his wife goes home to stay with his mother. One night he is overcome by his disappointment with the way his life had turned out and he begins arguing with God. It is one of those scenes that made even secular critics appreciate the movie. The mixture of love and anger — the revelation of a genuine relationship between the preacher and God — is remarkable.

Others have hinted of this part of our relationship with God. Geoffrey Wainwright cites the "strange" experience of wrestling with God as an expression of our personal involvement with him. Further he says that "the mysterious story of Jacob's night-long wrestling with the unnamed divine adversary at Penuel *(The face of God)* and his own acquisition of a new name of Israel *(He who strives with God, or God strives)* has continued to haunt the religious imagination and to provide the language for describing many a personal experience in prayer" *(Doxology)*.

The personal experience in prayer that Wainwright speaks of is often one that is full of emotion; not only love and adoration, but perplexity and anger. Certainly David is placing a very pointed question before the Lord when he declares:

> Why dost thou stand afar off, O LORD?
>> Why dost thou hide thyself in times of
>>> trouble?
> In arrogance the wicked hotly pursue the
>> poor; . . .
>
> — PSALM 10:1-2

> How long, O LORD? Wilt thou forget me for ever?
>> How long wilt thou hide thy face from me?

How long must I bear pain in my soul,
    and have sorrow in my heart all the day?
How long shall my enemy be exalted over me?
                         — *Psalm 13:1-3*

Rouse thyself! Why sleepest thou, O Lord?
    Awake! Do not cast us off for ever.
Why dost thou hide thy face?
    Why dost thou forget our affliction and
        oppression?
For our soul is bowed down to the dust;
    our body cleaves to the ground.
                         — *Psalm 44:23-25*

God is quite big enough to handle our real feelings. I'm not suggesting that we ought to rail against God, or shake our fists at Jesus in order to be authentic Christians. What I am suggesting is that God can handle our honesty. He has not abandoned us, and he will not abandon us because we have feelings that alarm us. God isn't alarmed, and he isn't caught off guard by our emotional life.

As we can see from just the few passages of the Psalms quoted above, David was serious about an honest relationship with God. Remember that it was David of whom it was said that he was a man after God's own heart (cf. 1 Samuel 13:14). Might this at least, in part, refer to his tenacity in holding on to his relationship with God?

Why Does God Permit Evil?

Another approach to anger toward God is more philosophical. How might we *understand* our experience of evil and injustice? The thinking Catholic has to process his or her experience intellectually. We Catholics have a real problem with the existence of evil. We are traditional monotheists. We believe that there is one God who is all-powerful and all-loving. He has revealed himself to us through the prophets and patriarchs of the Old Testament and most completely through his own Son, Jesus Christ. But here is our problem: Evil is part of life. We have "physical evil": evil that comes upon us through nature, like tornadoes, floods, famine, and disease. Then there is "moral evil": evil that comes upon us through other human beings. Our problem is, "Why does God permit any evil at all?" If God is indeed all-powerful and all-loving, it doesn't make sense that evil should exist at all. Could he have made a world without evil? If so, why didn't he do it?

One may come to the conclusion that God either lacks the power or the will to perform the good. In other words he can't be both all-powerful and all-loving and permit evil. Experience in life forces us to conclude that "divine justice" is hard to come by. Since our understanding of the Christian story doesn't square with the reality of experience, confusion and anger are natural responses. Catholic theologians have struggled with this issue from the very beginning and before them Jewish prophets and teachers tried to understand how an all-knowing and all-loving God could permit so many bad things to happen to his people. Job's suffering and Psalm 73 are but two examples of Israel's struggle with the apparent absence of divine justice.

Theodicies, explanations of why evil exists, have something in common with proofs for the existence of God. They are both intelligent attempts to give constructive explanations to problems that tend to be more useful to believers than to nonbelievers. I don't think I have ever personally known anyone who was converted to belief in God by intellectual argument. Believers want to give a reasoned account for their beliefs in the face of contrary evidence and within the context of an often hostile world. But few nonbelievers are convinced.

Ludwig Wittgenstein, the German philosopher, made a good point concerning belief in God and argumentation: "Believers . . . would never have come to believe as a result of such proofs [proofs for the existence of God]. . . . Life can educate one to a belief in God. And experiences too are what bring this about: but I don't mean visions and other forms of sense experience which show us the 'existence of this being,' but, e.g. sufferings of various sorts. These neither show us God in the way a sense impression shows us an object, nor do they give rise to conjectures about him. Experiences, thoughts — life can force this concept on us" *(The Christian Theology Reader)*.

I believe that a very similar line of thought can be applied to theodicies. They don't convince the unbeliever, but we are driven, as intelligent, thinking believers, to give a reasoned account of real-life experience.

So why do bad things happen to good people? Why is evil in the world? Catholics have traditionally given several explanations.

First, there is the argument from free will. God populated his creation with beings who have free will. They are not robots. They have the capacity to make choices, and when they make choices, sin becomes a possibility. Thus, according to tradition, Satan made a choice to turn away from God. He exalted himself. He chose his own will over God's will. In the Garden of Eden, Adam and Eve were confronted with personal, palpable, weighty evil in the Tempter. This manifestation of evil had a plan of action. It was intentional and it had a goal. It was organized and plotting. And it preexisted Adam and Eve. However, God did not create Satan. Satan created himself by using his free will to revolt against God. Adam and Eve followed suit. They, too, used their free will to rebel against God. And as we have all learned over and over since then, no one practices evil alone and in a disconnected state. Thus, all of creation was affected by the fall of man.

Our relationship to creation was like the beautiful, shimmering spiderwebs that we can find on chilly fall mornings in the South. Some are huge and intricately woven across rosebushes, shrubs, and picket fences. Dew hangs from the web like tiny silver beads. They are beautiful to look at, but if you touch a strand even slightly, the whole of the web will quiver and the beads of dew drop away, leaving a torn web. Thus did sin rend our relationship to creation.

We have an image in Genesis 3 and Romans 8 of a fallen and dying creation. This is what St. Paul was referring to when he said, "Therefore as sin came into the world through one man [Adam] and death through sin, and so death spread to all men because all men sinned . . ." (Romans 5:12).

But the process of death was itself destroyed by the Incarnation. So St. Paul completes the thought he began in Romans: "Then as one man's trespass led to condemnation for all men, so one man's action of righteousness leads to acquittal and life for all men. For as by one man's disobedience many were made sinners, so by one man's obedience many will be made righteous" (Romans 5:18-19).

In Romans 8:18-27 we have an image of the created order in "bondage to decay," but she is said to be "groaning," that is, she experiences both the pangs of death and of birth: the death of death and the birth of the kingdom of God where all creation will experience perfect liberty.

Thus, God is reweaving the web of life. Though we live with the present reality of death, Catholic Christians also live for the future realization of the kingdom of God when Jesus will wipe away all our tears, and death will be no more. So from this point of view the evil we live with today has its origin in the free will of the creature.

Another explanation that has been put forth over the years is that evil is an illusion of the limited created order we inhabit. What we call "evil" is simply part of the plan that we cannot understand. From God's point of view evil simply doesn't exist. We are like children trying to understand adult situations without the advantage of the adult experience. As C. S. Lewis once pointed out, if we tell a child that marriage represents a wonderful physical experience, the child may conjure up images of eating chocolate candy. So it is with our attempts to understand the inscrutable actions of God. As we attain a higher knowledge we will see that what we call evil is part of a grand plan and isn't evil at all.

Similar thinking occurs in some of the early gnostic heresies and in the Eastern religions. Carl Jung seems to have held to a position close to this. This point of view is obviously neither biblical nor Catholic, taken as it is. However, it is useful to keep in mind that we are finite, and often with experience and the perspective of age we can discover a higher point of view that gives some perspective on evil without denying its rebellious, destructive reality.

This mature perspective begins with the affirmation that evil is quite real. The stakes are high. As Flannery O'Connor put it when speaking of her art, "The Christian novelist is distinguished from his pagan colleagues by recognizing sin as sin. According to his heritage he sees it not as sickness or an accident of environment, but as a responsible choice of offense against God which involves his eternal future." Evil is not illusion. The most horrific evil imaginable was portrayed before the eyes of all creation in the Cross. But that's not all to be said about evil. For one thing, God seems to delight in bringing good out of evil. As horrific as the Cross was, God used it to save his dying creation.

Often time is required to take us to this higher stand-point. Take, for example, Joseph's attitude toward his long-lost brothers when he finally reveals his identity to them in Egypt. From their perspective they had fallen into the hands of the brother they had sinned against horribly. But Joseph had a different perspective: "You meant it for evil, God meant it for good" (cf. Genesis 50:20). In all likelihood Joseph did not always have that attitude. When he was thrown naked into the pit and then sold into slavery by his brothers, he probably did not understand his life as something God meant for good. He was probably not repeating over and over again, like a mantra, "They meant it for evil, God meant it for good." When he was in Pharaoh's prison and facing the possibility of being executed, he was probably not looking at things from that point of view. But his perspective did change, and at the end he had come to an understanding of God's character and actions that allowed him to proclaim mercy to his trembling and fearful brothers: "What you meant for evil, God meant for good."

This is the perspective of St. Paul's announcement to the Romans, "We know that in everything God works for good with those who love him" (Romans 8:28). The *Catechism of the Catholic Church* cites St. Thomas More's moving statement to his daughter just before his martyrdom: "Nothing can come but that that God wills. And I make me very sure that whatsoever that be, seem it never so bad in sight, it shall indeed be the best [*The Correspondence of Sir Thomas More*, . . . letter 206, lines 661-663]" (No. 313). Evil is very real. It is not an illusion. But our perspective on evil can change radically by the grace of God.

In this century, one other explanation has been attempted by some well-meaning theologians — some Christian and some Jewish — and that is the proposition that evil exists because God is not all-powerful. This is the position of thinkers who believe that God is in a state of becoming rather than being. God is in a state of growth. He isn't the same yesterday, today, and forever, because he has in a sense "evolved" himself. Therefore God isn't in any meaningful sense all-powerful or all-loving. This is the position that Rabbi Kushner takes in his book *Why Bad Things Happen to Good People*. It is also the position of thinkers like Alfred North Whitehead, a founder of process philosophy around the turn of the century, and John Cobb, a Protestant theologian who was especially committed to this position. A few years ago, Richard Swinburne, professor of philosophy and theology at Oxford, published a little book entitled *Is There A God?* In this book he strongly affirms the existence of a personal, theistic God, but one who is quite limited in what he can accomplish. The problem with process theology is that it isn't biblical and it isn't Catholic. The God of the Bible, the Holy Trinity, is God Almighty. In the Greek Orthodox Church he is often referred to as Pantocrator — King of the Universe. The solution of the process theologians simply gives too much away. It essentially jettisons the Catholic faith.

The last explanation of how evil can coexist with an all-powerful, all-loving God, is that there are no reasoned explanations to be had in this life. In a sense we return here to Wittgenstein's criticism of traditional arguments for the existence of God. We approach the problem of evil from within the radical Christian context of the Church and our belief in the Incarnation. Nicholas Arseniev, who taught theology at St. Vladimir's Orthodox Theological Seminary, compassionately points out that theoretical explanations don't comfort the troubled and broken heart.

Arseniev says that it is only with the "manifestation of a Higher Reality" — the suffering God of Christianity — that the human heart is quieted: "The Christian answer is the message about the Suffering God, or rather more than that: His really having come to share our suffering unto the depths of the death, and that on the Cross. This sheds a new light on the whole question, and not only on this question, but on the whole reality of the world's life. There is no explanation coming first, there is this fact coming first: He is sharing our suffering, He is hallowing our suffering — by His presence, by His participation therein. No explanation, but a new revelation. Something totally new, astonishing, incomprehensible, taking us totally aback, paradoxical and unexpected, and — true. And here lies that answer, not the theoretical answer — I mean, in the first place — but the practical, the real solution of the problem. His death and His suffering on the Cross are the real solution [to] the problem" *(Revelation of Life Eternal)*.

For the Church, belief in the incarnation of the God "who was once far off" changes everything. We can't go back to square one even if we wanted too. The God "who was once far off" has become one of us. The Catholic's answer to *What If God Was One of Us?* (Joan Osborn's popular ballad) is: He *is*. Not was, but is and always will be one of us, for us, "sharing our suffering . . . hallowing our suffering by His Presence, by His participation therein."

Appendix

Establishing a Grief Group in the Parish

The parish is the place where most Catholics live out their Catholic lives. It should also be the place where grieving Catholics can receive comfort, support, and healing. Many parishes have developed small "grief groups" for this purpose. Those who have recently experienced serious loss come together for a time of sharing and fellowship. Very often, these grief groups are a place where healing can be experienced, and wounded people can move toward wholeness within a sacramental and communal Catholic setting.

Here I will present two sections of material. The first section consists of practical experience I have gained from being involved in parish-based grief groups for many years. The material in the second section is drawn from theology and psychology — the two disciplines in which I have been trained. I will attempt to show that healing from loss, as the psychologists understand it, is enhanced by the experience in a grief group rooted in a Catholic Christian context.

Establishing a Small Grief Group

The first thing we have to do in order to get a grief group off the ground is to visit with our priest and introduce him to the idea. The pastoral benefits for the parish are great.

Roman Catholic parishes today, especially in high-growth suburban areas and the growing parts of the West and the South, are often mega-parishes. They are simply impossible to maintain from a pastoral point of view. A small group enhances the pastoral reach of the parish in three ways.

First, it will provide individual Catholics an opportunity to develop the priesthood of the believer — something that Protestants often claim as their exclusive territory. The group members learn how they are members of the Body of Christ, as opposed to members on a church roll. They really can help one another.

Second, groups are effective. They provide an excellent way for people in need of help to receive the counseling and care for healing. Groups are especially effective in reaching people who will avoid anything that smacks of formal, one-on-one counseling from a priest, social worker, or psychologist.

Third, groups make the most efficient use of the priest's, deacon's, nun's, or lay counselor's time. By using small groups in his parish the priest is multiplying his pastoral ministry.

Small groups employ what Father Ivan Clubberbuck, an English theologian, calls a "lay apostolate strategy." By developing lay leaders who can take groups and grow them, the pastor is multiplying pastoral resources exponentially. Of course, the pastor needs to care for his small groups and the people who lead them. He should develop some program of continuing education in the parish or the diocese for his group leaders, and he should develop some way of having regular meetings with them to talk about how to improve the groups, solve problems, and maintain priestly oversight. But the effort is worthwhile.

Finding Members

Advertise the grief support group. Parish bulletins are good, but unless the item of interest is pointed out in some way it often goes unnoticed. Ask your priest to announce the formation of the group during announcements on Sunday morning. Make sure that you list two contact persons with phone numbers and e-mail addresses, if possible. Posters and even a bulletin board or part of a bulletin board dedicated to grief and loss are useful in spreading the word.

Another source of potential participants is the core of interested persons — usually two or three — who are helping form the group. They all have friends who have experienced a loss. The core group in the parish will be aware of people who are suffering from loss. It is critical that you and your priest work hand in hand. So you will want to include him in any formation meetings and make sure that he is supportive.

Be prompt and welcoming in contacting people who express interest. A phone call is the most direct and usually successful approach, but a letter or note through the mail is often useful and it has the added benefit of giving the person a little breathing room before making a decision. Still, even this method is best followed up with a phone call or a personal face-to-face visit.

Find the Right Place to Meet
Sometimes a meeting room is not as easily found as one would think. Many organizations, classes, and already existing support groups are vying for the same space. So it is important to get started as soon as possible in order to secure a spot on the parish calendar. The parish church is an excellent neutral location for the group; but if that is not possible, other places are useful. Many communities have meeting rooms that can be scheduled, and we can always go to a home, although that should be a last resort. It is more difficult to maintain leadership, order, and confidentiality in a private home than in a neutral meeting place like the parish church.

If you provide baby-sitting services to the group, make sure that the room where the children are going to be kept is not next to the room you will be using for your grief group. Nothing can be more distracting and detrimental to a group than crying babies and children who are allowed to wander in and out of your meeting. The meeting room needs to be private. An atrium in the middle of a well-traveled parish hall, out in the open, for example, will not do. It eliminates the safety zone that the parishioners need in order to open up their grief to one another. Hopefully, the room will be furnished with comfortable furniture that can be arranged so that the focus is on the group.

Keep the Small Group "Small"

In order to maintain orderliness and to achieve the benefits of a small group, it is critical that the group remain small. Between eight and twelve participants is best. We can certainly begin with smaller groups. I have led groups with three and four participants; that may be necessary to get it off the ground. Don't let the smallness stop you. But in groups larger than twelve (I personally think eight is perfect), it becomes very difficult for all participants to have some time to talk about their concerns. Not having enough time to talk can become frustrating to group members and lead to dropout.

What Is Said in the Group Stays in the Group

The group must maintain confidentiality within the group. As group members learn to live together in an open, trusting environment, confidentiality will be honored as a spiritual exercise. New members who enter into a covenant with the existing group ought to be given this principle up front. Incidentally, this principle of not repeating anything outside the group is also part of the AA program.

Leadership Is the Critical Issue

Leaders lead by example — modeling, listening, and compassion, affirming the virtues of growth, as well as the pain of the loss. Leaders don't have to fix people and are not expected to. Leaders ought to have enough experience so that they aren't shaken by anger and deep sadness expressed by members of the group.

The pastor is the ideal person to begin the group, since he would have had some training in group work in the seminary. But it doesn't take long for lay leaders to be trained, and the pastor can usually do this himself or arrange for some diocesan workshops. The method we are recommending assumes that the laity will eventually step into the leadership role. The "model meeting" we are describing can actually be used as a guide for leading a group.

Here are a few "rules for leaders":

❀ Lead by telling your story.

❀ Don't let people monopolize the group's time.

❀ Use the telephone and mail to follow up.

❀ Refer people with complicated spiritual and emotional problems to the priest or a professional therapist.

❀ Begin and end on time. A meeting length of an hour and a half should suffice.

Setting Up and Welcoming

The group leader or leaders should arrive first — at least forty-five minutes before the others. Coffee and soft drinks should be supplied. I would suggest that the group go no further than coffee and soft drinks for refreshments. If a group begins to provide food or desserts it can quickly develop into a competition and distraction from the meeting. Keep it simple. Seating in a circle often works best to achieve a comfortable, welcoming setting for the group.

The group leader or leaders should greet the participants as they arrive, introduce them to one another, and allow them to get acquainted. The group leader should not be the center of attention. Like a good parent, he or she must delight in the growth of the members and the group itself. Over time the group will come to resemble a family in many ways. The group leader is the leader. He or she is the one who says it is time to start, and the best time to start is at the time advertised. And the best time to end is when you say you are going to end. For a group with eight to ten participants meeting once a week, one-and-a-half hours is enough time. End on time with the group standing while the Lord's Prayer is recited. That builds confidence in the group leader and it lets the people know that the rest of their life is important and respected as well. You might let folks know that if they wish, they can linger for a while longer after the meeting is officially over.

Getting Started

There are many ways to start a meeting like this. I like to start by reading from a sheet of paper containing the Serenity Prayer, the group's mission statement, an applicable selection of Scripture, and the Lord's Prayer. Pass that sheet of paper out to the participants and ask them to stand and pray the Serenity Prayer together. After the prayer, ask someone to read the mission statement and discuss the rules of the group — for example, the rule of confidentiality. The mission statement should be read at every meeting even if it isn't discussed. It only takes a minute or two and it helps maintain the focus of the group.

At the first few meetings you might want to see if there is some discussion of the mission statement itself. The group leader should also plan on laying down the ground rules for the group. The leader and the priest will have to decide whether or not they will allow the mission statement to be changed by the group. There is some real value in having the group construct its own mission statement, though at some point the mission statement needs to be fixed and unchangeable. Once that is done, it becomes the touchstone for judging whether or not the group is actually accomplishing what it needs to accomplish. Any member of the group has the right to point to the mission statement when he or she feels that the group is moving away from its job. If the group is going to have a very specific purpose — for instance, helping parishioners who have lost family members through violence — that should be included in the mission statement.

Here is a generalized model of a mission statement that you may use and change to fit your particular needs in your parish:

> The mission of St. Stephen's Parish Grief and Loss Support Group is to bring together brothers and sisters who are living with a difficult loss for the purpose of mutual support, education, encouragement, and fellowship. Our only purpose for existing is to incarnate St. Paul's statement to the Corinthians: "Blessed be the God and Father of our Lord Jesus Christ, a gentle Father and the God of all consolation, who comforts us in all our sorrows, so that we can offer others, in their sorrows, the consolation that we have received from God ourselves." We acknowledge that we are a diverse group of Catholics and that our losses are different. But we also acknowledge that each of us has gone or is going through very similar emotional, spiritual, social, and physical stages as we try to live with our loss. We are not professionals, but we are all knowledgeable through personal experience of the effects of loss. With the agreement of the group we may use professionals for the purpose of education and to help us better learn to support one another. We

intend to do no harm, but only to provide a safe place with compassionate friends who know something of what we have experienced. We acknowledge our complete dependence upon God and the Catholic Church for our well-being.

The Serenity Prayer

God grant me the serenity
To accept the things I cannot change,
Courage to change the things I can,
And wisdom to know the difference.

Selected Scriptures

"And his gifts were that some should be apostles, some prophets, some evangelists, some pastors and teachers; for the equipment of the saints, for the work of ministry, for building up the body of Christ, until we all attain to the unity of the faith and of the knowledge of the Son of God, to mature manhood, to the measure of the stature of the fullness of Christ . . ." (Ephesians 4:11-13).

"Blessed are those who mourn, for they shall be comforted" (Matthew 5:4).

"Blessed be the God and Father of our Lord Jesus Christ, the Father of mercies and God of all comfort, who comforts us in all our affliction, so that we may be able to comfort those who are in affliction, with the comfort with which we ourselves are comforted by God. For as we share abundantly in Christ's sufferings, so through Christ we share abundantly in comfort too" (2 Corinthians 1:3-5).

Storytelling and Discussion

More times than I can remember, one or two group members begin to weep or are teary-eyed as soon as these opening readings are finished. This is often an indication that they are ready to say something about their loss.

The group leader may simply inquire of that person in a gentle and soft manner: "Robert, it seems that something about what we have read has touched you. Can you share that with the group?" The leader has to lead. Everyone has noticed the weeping and the teary eyes, but it is the leader that will softly and gently draw attention to that person and offer an opportunity to open up his or her grief to their friends. If the group members are not forthcoming with their own grief, one of the leaders might show why a grief group is important by sharing a story out of his or her own experience.

One person's story acts as a sort of catalyst for the stories of the other members. "Is Robert's story bringing up something that you would like to share with us?" is the kind of address the leader would want to make to a person who is moved by another's story. Once the group takes off, the members will begin to share more freely and offer a listening ear and sound Christian and psychological advice to the other members.

One critical piece for a successful group is that the leaders know their own limits. The support group is not a psychotherapy group led by a professional. It is for the building up of the Body of Christ and her members. It should always aim at becoming a lay-led group. But leaders have to know when they are over their heads and they have to be strong enough to bring the group back to its mission statement as a clarification of purpose and as a way to avoid getting into too deep psychological waters.

It is important for the leader or leaders to have had some prior experience in group work. This is another reason that having the priest as a leader can be helpful. His training in the seminary and often in the hospital has placed him in small-group situations throughout his career. And most of the time today the clergy member is required to have had Clinical Pastoral Education, a small-group experience that will help prepare him for leadership in small groups. He also knows his limits as a leader and counselor. He knows the importance of knowing when and where to draw the line and when to refer people out to professional counselors.

How Healing Happens in Small Groups

The Church has always known that small groups are good for people. Prayer circles, fellowship groups, Bible studies, choirs, and other gatherings of Christians have been around as long as there has been a Church.

Lately, small groups have proliferated throughout the secular world. In hospitals and psychologists' offices and in helping organizations like AA and Compassionate Friends, the small group has found a home. People have discovered that the small group provides a setting for recovery and reentry into life that is natural and charitable.

Why are small groups so helpful? It is worth taking a close look at this question. Even though we know *that* small groups work, it's helpful to know *why* they work — a perspective that will be useful for everyone leading a group of grieving people in a parish-based setting. In my experience, the secular world of psychotherapy casts much light on this rather mysterious question.

One of the fathers of the small-group movement in the world of psychotherapy is Irvin D. Yalom, professor of psychiatry at the Stanford University School of Medicine. In his research and practice of group psychotherapy, Yalom has formulated a set of basic therapeutic factors that represent the "core" of group therapy. These are present as well in effective parish-based grief support groups.

Before examining these factors, let's make one important clarification. There's a big difference between a grief support group based in a parish and composed of Christians and a group therapy group in a secular setting. The grief support group looks to the Lord; secular psychotherapy is ordinarily neutral on ultimate spiritual questions. I am not suggesting that we set up therapy groups in our parishes.

Nevertheless, all groups where healing takes place share some important things in common. The word "therapy" may be too clinical or secular for a parish setting, but the root of the word actually has a sound theological meaning. The Bible uses the Greek equivalent of the term "therapy" to refer to healing and wholeness brought about by Jesus' ministry. Our Lord's death and passion are cited by the Apostle for their "therapeutic" effect upon our relationship with God: "With his stripes we are healed" (Isaiah 53:5). The "healing" that the Apostles refer to constantly throughout the New Testament is often physical and emotional and always deeply spiritual. Our broken relationships with God and one another are healed by the Cross. We can view these "therapeutic factors" as opportunities for spiritual healing as well. Many of us will be surprised at just how clearly spiritual many of these core elements are. As the reader will see, what Yalom calls a "therapeutic factor" the Church will understand from a decidedly theological and spiritual point of view.

Let's examine ten therapeutic factors identified by Yalom in his research and see how they might work in a parish-based grief support group. The ten factors are:

* instillation of hope
* universality
* imparting of information
* altruism
* corrective recapitulation of the primary family group

- ❀ development of socializing techniques
- ❀ imitative behavior
- ❀ catharsis
- ❀ existential factors
- ❀ cohesiveness

Instillation of Hope

Therapy groups instill hope in patients who are demoralized and pessimistic about therapy, says Yalom. People gain hope from observing others, especially others with similar problems, who have profited from therapy.

This fits hand in glove with a Catholic understanding of mutual support within the Body of Christ, as St. Paul so aptly put it when writing to the Church in Corinth (cf. 2 Corinthians 1:3-5).

When we can authentically say, "I know just how you feel," we are introducing a powerful healing presence into the life of a grieving person. Some therapists argue that we don't know "just how they feel" — that each person is unique in his or her loss and in that person's feelings about it. While technically true, the objection is greatly exaggerated. Obviously we haven't experienced the precise loss of our neighbor. But if we listen in a small group, they will tell us about their loss. And at the right time we can help.

One way we help is simply by sharing the hope that we have regained ourselves. Few things can be more paralyzing than the loss of hope. Loss of hope for renewal, happiness, and a productive life is often the subjective experience of the person who has suffered a significant loss. If we have been through the valley of the shadow of death and come out the other side, we know that there is an "other side."

The hope we instill as Catholics is not "I hope so," but rather "I have a confident expectation." Ours is not a "hope-so religion," but rather one of looking to the future in expectation. But even Catholics go through the dark night of the soul. So there are two kinds of hope that we are talking about here. One is the hope that says things can and will get better. The other is more specifically Catholic in that the reason we have confidence that things can and will get better is because we believe in Jesus Christ. That is theological hope.

Universality

"Patients often enter therapy with the disquieting feeling that they are unique in their misery," says Yalom. In group therapy, they hear others share similar concerns and they understand that they are not alone. This usually comes as a welcome relief.

In grief, especially, the feelings of anger and relief can be somewhat bewildering. Grieving people often feel unique in their sorrow, and this is alienating. Feelings of uniqueness separate us from the rest of the human race. "I am alone. No one has ever felt this way before." However, these experiences are universal. Many people have felt this way before. It is truly blessed to be able to spend time with others who have had similar experiences.

Christians can turn to the example of the Lord. When we want to clam up and nurse feelings of being unusual and strange, when we think that we don't belong anywhere, consider all the "unusual and strange" people that Jesus welcomed into his life: Mary Magdalene; Zacchaeus; Matthew, a hated tax-collector; and the ever-processing host of diseased, maimed, disfigured, and unclean persons. From Jesus' point of view, these were all God's children for whom he had come. No one is too strange, diseased, disfigured, or unclean that Jesus cannot heal with his touch. We can bring those feelings of strangeness and aloneness to the small grief support group. The group can welcome us into the family of God — where we are not alone.

Imparting of Information

Says Yalom in his book *Inpatient Group Psychotherapy*: "Therapy groups implicitly or explicitly provide information to the members." (Incidentally, all subsequent excerpts by this author will be from this particular book of his.) Says Scripture: "Get wisdom; get insight. / Do not forsake her, and she will keep you; / love her, and she will guard you" (Proverbs 4:5-6); "He taught them as one who had authority" (Mark 1:22).

Groups give their members valuable information about their condition. Therapy groups instruct about depression, anxiety, addiction, and all the other problems that afflict their members. So, too, with grief. Understanding how grief is organized in the human experience is critically important for grieving people.

Nevertheless, information must be imparted carefully. We don't want to press people's individual experience into a universalized mold. We have to be careful not to project the wrong conclusion onto a set of facts. Philip did this when Jesus asked him where they might find enough food to feed a crowd of five thousand. Philip looked around and said that the situation was hopeless — an erroneous conclusion, as Jesus demonstrated. We need to beware of doing the same with the facts of grief. However, over a period of time, people in the grief support group will have the opportunity to bring information to the group, to raise questions about grief, to explore personal insights, and to get clarification about their own experiences. Viewed this way, the grief group becomes a classroom where the immediate experience of bereavement can be understood and even used for our spiritual enrichment. This is part of the process of healing.

Altruism

Yalom describes altruism in group therapy in careful clinical language: "When patients who have completed group therapy are asked to look back over it, they invariably credit other members as having been important in their improvement. . . . To learn that one is able to be useful to others is a refreshing experience."

The New Testament puts it another way: "Little children, yet a little while I am with you. You will seek me; and as I said to the Jews so now I say to you, 'Where I am going you cannot come.' A new commandment I give to you, that you love one another; even as I have loved you, that you also love one another. By this all men will know that you are my disciples, if you have love for one another" (John 13:33-35). And again: "For here we have no lasting city, but we seek the city which is to come. Through him then let us continually offer up a sacrifice of praise to God, that is, the fruit of lips that acknowledge his name. Do not neglect to do good and to share what you have, for such sacrifices are pleasing to God" (Hebrews 13:14-16).

Here is a powerful Christian opportunity in the small group. The group provides us with a setting where we can exercise our love for the brethren in very specific, concrete ways. To express words of understanding and to enter into the horizon of another person's grief require a willingness to step outside of one's own self. It is an antidote to self-centeredness, what Yalom calls "morbid self-absorption." Often when we stop to help another person, to pass over to that person's standpoint of grief, we discover happiness for the first time in our lives. Often the road to recovery is a path that moves us away from self-absorption to focus upon other people and their needs. Of course, it is possible that a person could even abuse this. It can become a way to avoid what one needs to deal with in one's own life. But one of the values of the support group is that the other members usually pick up on that avoidance and then they can gently point it out and invite the avoider to step up to the plate, so to speak, and share.

Corrective Recapitulation of the Primary Family Group

"The group therapy situation resembles the early family in a number of ways, and patients have a tendency to reexperience old familial conflicts," writes Yalom. This happens in the support group as well, but we must be careful. In therapy, the therapist will challenge dysfunctional behavior and aim at corrective behavior. This is not the goal of a support group, and the group and its leader should resist the temptation to attempt it. A support group is not a therapy group.

However, they overlap, as we have already seen. Something like recapitulation of the primary family group could occur on a less therapeutic level even in a support group. Occasionally individuals in a group will link up in a way that seems to suggest something like this. For example, a young woman may develop a relationship of respect and compassion with an older woman; this can be a mother/daughter alliance forming. This kind of alliance can often be helpful as long as it stays on the level of support and caring. Intensive work on dysfunctional childhood patterns of behavior should ordinarily be done in therapy per se — not in a grief support group. But the two are not mutually exclusive. Grieving people can participate in both a support group and psychotherapy, time and energy permitting, and the two can support and reinforce each other.

Development of Socializing Techniques

"All therapy groups help patients develop social skills. Some groups do so explicitly by using such procedures as role playing, where members rehearse certain difficult social situations (for example, a job interview or asking for a date), while others offer constructive criticism," Yalom writes.

One of the most difficult stages of recovery from loss is reentry into life. Whether it is the loss of a job or the loss of a spouse, reentering life can be tricky, even harrowing. Social occasions after a major loss can become ordeals. It is not unusual for people to experience panic attacks as they attempt to reenter life.

In the safe setting of a grief support group, people can fully discuss their fears and misgivings about picking up a social life after the death of a spouse or some other significant loss. Indeed, it is just what we need. The decision to participate in a small group is in itself a concrete way to resume our social life. In a support group people can ask for and receive feedback about their feelings and behavior. This should be actively encouraged. Suggestions and criticisms from fellow group members boost confidence and give permission to enter into the deeper waters of a renewed life.

Of course, the suggestions and criticisms ought always to be constructive and not done in a critical or mean spirit. The question of role-playing should be handled by the leadership of the group. Some light role-playing with such issues as applying for a job, asking for a date, how to do small talk at a party, or how to give comfort to a person without sending the wrong messages about our intentions can be quite fruitful for the participants.

Imitative Behavior
Role-playing leads naturally to Yalom's seventh therapeutic factor: healing through imitating. "Therapy group members," he points out, "often model themselves upon aspects of other members as well as of the therapist. Even if the modeling is short-lived, the process of

trying out new behavior is an invaluable catalyst to un-freezing — that is, the dissolution of rigid patterns of behavior." This is true, he says, even for group members who do less work in the group. These individuals often gain some vicarious therapy by being in a group where others are working hard.

The application for a grief-and-loss group in a par-ish are self-evident. The grief experience has thrust us into a new and frightening world and our behavior is often negatively affected by that experience. Fear, guilt, and deep sadness over the loss may lead us to behave in unproductive ways. Some people act out in a negative and destructive way; others withdraw into a shell to pro-tect themselves. If the leaders bring healthy, spiritually wholesome attitudes and behaviors to the group, hurt-ing people can learn by watching and by imitation.

I vividly recall the change that occurred in one young woman in a group in precisely this way. She had experi-enced a major loss and then began acting out in de-structive behavior. Then she experienced compassion and understanding from her group leaders. She imitated this in her relationship with other members of the group and eventually showed them great compassion and under-standing. Healing of her own loss and consequent be-havior came this way.

Catharsis

The honest expression of feeling is important for healing. This is a crucial element of group therapy, ac-cording to Yalom. "The open expression and release of affect [that is, feeling or emotion] is an important part of the group therapeutic experience. But it is a partial pro-cess; sheer ventilation in itself is rarely of lasting ben-efit. What is of great importance is that the group mem-bers learn how to express feelings and that the expression of feelings is not socially calamitous."

There are two parts to catharsis. One is to have a safe place to ventilate feelings; the other is learning how to express feelings in a constructive ongoing manner. Having a safe place to vent one's spleen is particularly important within the bereavement experience. Grieving people typically experience feelings that are thought to be unacceptable — particularly feelings of anger, fear, and relief. If left unexpressed, these kinds of emotions and opinions can be deadly. Some social restraint is necessary in most situations. We don't go around expressing our most intimate feelings to everyone with whom we come into contact. But we do need an outlet to get potentially destructive feelings off our chest. The grief support group is that place.

The release of strong negative feelings and learning healthy ways of expressing our feelings is part of learning to live as a forgiven Catholic who has nothing to hide. The sacrament of reconciliation is part of this process as well.

Existential Factors

Therapy involves dealing with the "big questions" of the human condition. Yalom puts it this way: "The existential frame of reference in psychotherapy posits that, to a significant degree, anxiety and, hence, most psychopathology issue from the human being's confrontation with certain basic dimensions or 'ultimate concerns' of existence; death, freedom (responsibility and willing), isolation, and meaninglessness."

Here, of course, we are on our home turf as the Church. We have answers to these questions, though not because we have figured it out over time or even because we have holy men and women among us who have made these discoveries. We know the answers to these questions because God has come down from heaven and he has spoken to the Church face to face. Any group that is formed within a Catholic parish will have as its legacy the faith of the Church. Here is an opportunity for teaching and immediate application.

Cohesiveness

Healing involves being joined to humanity. Says Yalom: "Cohesiveness — the sense of 'groupness,' of being accepted, of being a valued member of a valued group — is the group therapy analogue of 'relationship' in individual therapy."

This corresponds to what we call *koinonia* in the Church. The word *koinonia* is usually translated "fellowship" or "brotherhood" in the English translations of the Bible. The Church has experienced this from the beginning as a supernatural gift from God. And yet how many Catholics experience anything that they would identify as "fellowship," within the parish?

For the Catholic, *koinonia* is realized in four ways. First, there is *koinonia* in our common spiritual birth through the sacrament of baptism in the Name of the Trinity. Second, there is *koinonia* in the Blessed Sacrament. We all partake of the same gift, from the same altar. The Blessed Sacrament binds us together as a sacramental brotherhood or family. Third, we have *koinonia* in the teaching of the Apostles. There is one faith, which is the teaching of the Apostles handed down to us through apostolic succession. Finally, we have the potential in small groups to experience an immediate cohesiveness, a sense of family belonging, that can be stronger because it rests upon the first three pillars of Christian fellowship.

Prayers for the Grieving

Serenity Prayer

God grant me the serenity
To accept the things I cannot change,
The courage to change the things I can,
And the wisdom to know the difference.
Living one day at a time,
Enjoying one moment at a time;
Accepting hardship as a pathway to peace;
Taking, as you did, O Lord Jesus,
This sinful world as it is,
Not as I would have it;
Trusting that you will make all things right
If I surrender to your will;
So that I may be reasonably happy in this life,
And supremely happy with you forever in the next.
Amen.

— ADAPTED FROM THE ORIGINAL *SERENITY PRAYER*
BY REINHOLD NIEBUHR

Various Prayers of Abandonment

Father,
I abandon myself into your hands;
do with me what you will.
Whatever you may do, I thank you;
I am ready for all; I accept all.
Let only your will be done in me
and in all your creatures —
I wish no more than this, O Lord.
Into your hands I commend my soul;
I offer it to you with all the love of my heart,
for I love you, Lord,
and so need to give myself,
to surrender myself into your hands

without reserve and with boundless confidence.
For you are my Father.

— CHARLES DE FOUCAULD

O Heart of Love, I place all my trust in Thee, for I
fear all things from my own weakness, but I hope for all
things from Thy goodness.

— ST. MARGARET MARY

I live through the mercy of Jesus, to whom I owe
everything and from whom I expect everything.

— POPE JOHN XXIII

Yet, O Lord, though I have no feeling of confidence
in You, nevertheless, I know that You are my God, that I
am all Yours, and that I have no hope but in Your goodness; so, I abandon myself entirely into Your hands.

— ST. FRANCIS DE SALES

You make a root below the soil flourish and you
can make fruitful the darkness in which you keep me.

— JEAN-PIERRE DE CAUSSADE

I adore all Thy purposes without knowing them; I
am silent; I offer myself in sacrifice; I yield myself to Thee;
I would have no other desire than to accomplish Thy
will. Teach me to pray; pray Thyself in me.

— FRANÇOIS FÉNELON

May I be patient! It is so difficult to realize what one
believes, and to make these trials, as they are intended,
real blessings.

— JOHN HENRY NEWMAN

My own heart let me more have pity on.

— GERARD MANLEY HOPKINS

Suffering

Blessed be the God and Father of our Lord Jesus Christ, the Father of mercies and God of all comfort, who comforts us in all our affliction, so that we may be able to comfort those who are in any affliction, with the comfort with which we ourselves are comforted by God. For as we share abundantly in Christ's sufferings, so through Christ we share abundantly in comfort too.

— *2 CORINTHIANS 1:3-5*

Come to me, all who labor and are heavy laden, and I will give you rest. Take my yoke upon you, and learn from me; for I am gentle and lowly in heart, and you will find rest for your souls. For my yoke is easy, and my burden is light.

— *MATTHEW 11:28-30*

So we do not lose heart. Though our outer nature is wasting away, our inner nature is being renewed every day. For this slight momentary affliction is preparing for us an eternal weight of glory beyond all comparison, because we look not to the things that are seen but to the things that are unseen; for the things that are seen are transient, but the things that are unseen are eternal.

— *2 CORINTHIANS 4:16-18*

For all who are led by the Spirit of God are sons of God. For you did not receive the spirit of slavery to fall back into fear, but you have received the spirit of sonship. When we cry, "Abba! Father!" it is the Spirit himself bearing witness with our spirit that we are children of God, and if children, then heirs, heirs of God and fellow heirs with Christ, provided we suffer with him in order that we may also be glorified with him.

I consider that the sufferings of this present time

are not worth comparing with the glory that is to be revealed to us.

— *Romans 8:14-18*

And after you have suffered a little while, the God of all grace, who has called you to his eternal glory in Christ, will himself restore, establish, and strengthen you.

— *1 Peter 5:10*

Comfort, we beseech thee, most gracious God, this thy servant, cast down and faint of heart amidst the sorrows and difficulties of the world; and grant that, by the power of thy Holy Spirit, he may be enabled to go upon his way rejoicing, and give thee continual thanks for thy sustaining providence; through Jesus Christ our Lord. Amen.

— *Book of Common Prayer*

O Lord, our heavenly Father, without Whom all purposes are frustrated, all efforts are vain, grant us the assistance of the Holy Spirit, that we may not sorrow as those without hope, but may now return to the duties of our present life with humble confidence in thy protection, and so govern our thoughts and actions that no business or work may ever withdraw our minds from Thee, but that in the changes of this life we may fix our hearts upon the reward which Thou hast promised to them that serve Thee, and that whatsoever things are true, whatsoever things are pure, whatsoever things are lovely, whatsoever things are of good report, wherein there is virtue, wherein there is praise, we may think upon and do, and obtain mercy, consolation, and everlasting happiness. Grant this, O Lord, for the sake of Jesus Christ. Amen.

— *Dr. Samuel Johnson, 1709*

For Those Who Suffer

> For those who suffer,
> and those who cry this night,
> give them repose, Lord;
> a pause in their burdens.
> Let there be minutes
> where they experience peace,
> not of man
> but of angels.
> Love them, Lord,
> when others cannot.
> Hold them, Lord,
> when we fail with human arms.
> Hear their prayers
> and give them the ability to hear You back
> in whatever language they best understand.
>
> — *ANONYMOUS*

Trust and Hope

Prayer of Solace

> May Christ support us all the day long,
> till the shadows lengthen,
> and the evening comes,
> and the busy world is hushed,
> and the fever of life is over
> and our work is done.
> Then in his mercy
> may he give us a safe lodging,
> and holy rest and peace at the last. Amen.
>
> — *ATTRIBUTED TO JOHN HENRY NEWMAN*

Who shall separate us from the love of Christ? Shall tribulation, or distress, or persecution, or famine, or nakedness, or peril, or sword? As it is written,

> "For thy sake we are being killed all the day long;
> we are regarded as sheep to be slaughtered."

No, in all these things we are more than conquerors through him who loved us. For I am sure that neither death, nor life, nor angels, nor principalities, nor things present, nor things to come, nor powers, nor height, nor depth, nor anything else in all creation, will be able to separate us from the love of God in Christ Jesus our Lord.

— *Romans 8:35-39*

Then I saw a new heaven and a new earth; for the first heaven and the first earth had passed away, and the sea was no more. And I saw the holy city, new Jerusalem, coming down out of heaven from God, prepared as a bride adorned for her husband; and I heard a great voice from the throne saying, "Behold, the dwelling of God is with men. He will dwell with them, and they shall be his people, and God himself will be with them; he will wipe away every tear from their eyes, and death shall be no more, neither shall there be mourning nor crying nor pain any more, for the former things have passed away."

And he who sat upon the throne said, "Behold, I make all things new."

— *Revelation 21:1-5*

He who dwells in the shelter of the Most High,
    who abides in the shadow of the Almighty,
will say to the LORD, "My refuge and my fortress;
    my God, in whom I trust."
For he will deliver you from the snare of the fowler
    and from the deadly pestilence;
he will cover you with his pinions,
    and under his wings you will find refuge;
    his faithfulness is a shield and buckler.
You will not fear the terror of the night,
    nor the arrow that flies by day,

nor the pestilence that stalks in darkness,
  nor the destruction that wastes at noonday.
A thousand may fall at your side,
  ten thousand at your right hand;
  but it will not come near you.
You will only look with your eyes
  and see the recompense of the wicked.
Because you have made the LORD your refuge,
  the Most High your habitation,
no evil shall befall you,
  no scourge come near your tent.
For he will give his angels charge of you
  to guard you in all your ways.
On their hands they will bear you up,
  lest you dash your foot against a stone
You will tread on the lion and the adder,
  the young lion and the serpent you will
    trample under foot.
Because he cleaves to me in love, I will deliver him;
  I will protect him, because he knows my
    name.
When he calls to me, I will answer him;
  I will be with him in trouble,
  I will rescue him and honor him.
With long life I will satisfy him,
  and show him my salvation.

— *PSALM 91*

For Those We Love

Almighty God, we entrust all who are dear to us
to thy never-failing care and love, for this life and
  the life to come; knowing that thou art doing
    for them
better things than we can desire or pray for; through
Jesus Christ our Lord. Amen.

— *BOOK OF COMMON PRAYER*

Forgiveness

What man of you, having a hundred sheep, if he has lost one of them, does not leave the ninety-nine in the wilderness, and go after the one which is lost, until he finds it? And when he has found it, he lays it on his shoulders, rejoicing. And when he comes home, he calls together his friends and his neighbors, saying to them, "Rejoice with me, for I have found my sheep which was lost." Just so, I tell you, there will be more joy in heaven over one sinner who repents than over ninety-nine righteous persons who need no repentance.

— *Luke 15:4-7*

Have mercy on me, O God,
    according to thy steadfast love;
    according to thy abundant mercy blot out my
      transgressions.
Wash me thoroughly from my iniquity,
    and cleanse me from my sin!
For I know my transgressions,
    and my sin is ever before me.
Against thee, thee only, have I sinned,
    and done that which is evil in thy sight,
so that thou art justified in thy sentence
    and blameless in thy judgment.
Behold, I was brought forth in iniquity,
    and in sin did my mother conceive me.
Behold, thou desirest truth in the inward being;
    therefore teach me wisdom in my secret
      heart.
Purge me with hyssop, and I shall be clean;
    wash me, and I shall be whiter than snow.
Fill me with joy and gladness;
    let the bones which thou hast broken rejoice.
Hide thy face from my sins,
    and blot out all my iniquities.

Create in me a clean heart, O God,
   and put a new and right spirit within me.
Cast me not away from thy presence,
   and take not thy holy Spirit from me.
Restore to me the joy of thy salvation,
   and uphold me with a willing spirit.
Then I will teach transgressors thy ways,
   and sinners will return to thee.
Deliver me from bloodguiltiness, O God,
      thou God of my salvation,
   and my tongue will sing aloud of thy
      deliverance.
O Lord, open thou my lips,
   and my mouth shall show forth thy praise.
For thou hast no delight in sacrifice;
      were I to give a burnt offering, thou wouldst
      not be pleased.
The sacrifice acceptable to God is a broken spirit;
      a broken and contrite heart, O God, thou wilt
      not despise.
Do good to Zion in thy good pleasure;
   rebuild the walls of Jerusalem,
then wilt thou delight in right sacrifices,
      in burnt offerings and whole burnt offerings;
      then bulls will be offered on thy altar.
                                    — *Psalm 51*

Act of Contrition
   O my God, I am heartily sorry
   for having offended you,
   and I detest all my sins,
   because of your just punishments,
   but most of all because they offend you, my God,
   who are all-good and deserving of all love.
   I firmly resolve,
   with the help of your grace,

to sin no more
and to avoid the occasions of sin.

— *Traditional*

Psalms for the Grieving

Psalm 23

The LORD is my shepherd, I shall not want;
    he makes me lie down in green pastures.
He leads me beside still waters;
    he restores my soul.
He leads me in paths of righteousness
    for his name's sake.
Even though I walk through the valley of the
    shadow of death,
      I fear no evil;
for thou art with me;
    thy rod and thy staff,
    they comfort me.
Thou preparest a table before me
    in the presence of my enemies;
thou anointest my head with oil,
    my cup overflows.
Surely goodness and mercy shall follow me
    all the days of my life;
and I shall dwell in the house of the LORD
    for ever.

Psalm 27

The LORD is my light and my salvation;
    whom shall I fear?
The LORD is the stronghold of my life;
    of whom shall I be afraid?
When evildoers assail me,
    uttering slanders against me,
my adversaries and foes,
    they shall stumble and fall.

Though a host encamp against me,
　　my heart shall not fear;
though war arise against me,
　　yet I will be confident.
One thing have I asked of the LORD,
　　that will I seek after;
that I may dwell in the house of the LORD
　　all the days of my life,
to behold the beauty of the LORD,
　　and to inquire in his temple.
For he will hide me in his shelter
　　in the day of trouble;
he will conceal me under the cover of his tent,
　　he will set me high upon a rock.
And now my head shall be lifted up
　　above my enemies round about me;
and I will offer in his tent
　　sacrifices with shouts of joy;
I will sing and make melody to the LORD.
Hear, O LORD, when I cry aloud,
　　be gracious to me and answer me!
Thou hast said, "Seek ye my face."
　　My heart says to thee,
"Thy face, LORD, do I seek."
　　Hide not thy face from me.
Turn not thy servant away in anger,
　　thou who hast been my help.
Cast me not off, forsake me not,
　　O God of my salvation!
For my father and my mother have forsaken me,
　　but the LORD will take me up.
Teach me thy way, O LORD;
　　and lead me on a level path
　　because of my enemies.
Give me not up to the will of my adversaries;
　　for false witnesses have risen against me,

and they breathe out violence.
I believe that I shall see the goodness of the LORD
 in the land of the living!
Wait for the LORD;
 be strong, and let your heart take courage;
 yea, wait for the LORD!

Psalm 46

God is our refuge and strength,
 a very present help in trouble.
Therefore we will not fear though the earth
 should change,
  though the mountains shake in the heart of
   the sea;
though its waters roar and foam,
  though the mountains tremble with its
   tumult.
There is a river whose streams make glad
 the city of God,
  the holy habitation of the Most High.
God is in the midst of her, she shall not be moved;
 God will help her right early.
The nations rage, the kingdoms totter;
 he utters his voice, the earth melts.
The LORD of hosts is with us;
 the God of Jacob is our refuge.
Come, behold the works of the LORD,
 how he has wrought desolations in the earth.
He makes wars cease to the end of the earth;
 he breaks the bow, and shatters the spear,
 he burns the chariots with fire!
"Be still, and know that I am God.
 I am exalted among the nations,
 I am exalted in the earth!"
The LORD of hosts is with us;
 the God of Jacob is our refuge.

Psalm 121

I lift up my eyes to the hills.
 From whence does my help come?
My help comes from the Lord,
 who made heaven and earth.
He will not let your foot be moved,
 he who keeps you will not slumber.
Behold, he who keeps Israel
 will neither slumber nor sleep.
The Lord is your keeper;
 the Lord is your shade
 on your right hand.
The sun shall not smite you by day,
 nor the moon by night.
The Lord will keep you from all evil;
 he will keep your life.
The Lord will keep
 your going out and your coming in
 from this time forth and for evermore.

Psalm 130

Out of the depths I cry to thee, O Lord!
 Lord, hear my voice!
Let thy ears be attentive
 to the voice of my supplications!
If thou, O Lord, shouldst mark iniquities,
 Lord, who could stand?
But there is forgiveness with thee,
 that thou mayest be feared.
I wait for the Lord, my soul waits,
 and in his word I hope;
my soul waits for the Lord
 more than watchmen for the morning,
 more than watchmen for the morning.
O Israel, hope in the Lord!
 For with the Lord there is steadfast love,

and with him is plenteous redemption.
And he will redeem Israel
from all his iniquities.

Prayers for the Dead

In Loving Memory

Almighty God, through the death of your Son on the cross, you have overcome death for us. Through his burial and resurrection from the dead you have made the grave a holy place and restored us to eternal life. We pray for those who died believing in Jesus and are buried with him in the hope of rising again. God of the living and the dead, may those who faithfully believed in you on earth praise you for ever in the joy of heaven. We ask this through Christ our Lord. Amen.

— *Traditional*

Into thy hands, O merciful Saviour, we commend the soul of thy servant, now departed from the body. Acknowledge, we humbly beseech thee, a sheep of thine own fold, a lamb of thine own flock, a sinner of thine own redeeming. Receive him into the arms of thy mercy, into the blessed rest of everlasting peace, and into the glorious company of the saints in light.

— *Book of Common Prayer*

O Lord, by Whom all souls live; we thank Thee for those whom Thy love has called from the life of trial to the life of rest. We trust them to Thy care; we pray Thee that by Thy grace we may be brought to enjoy with them in endless life Thy glory; through Jesus Christ our Lord. Amen.

— *Traditional*

On the Anniversary of a Death

Lord God,
you are the glory of believers

and the life of the just.
Your Son redeemed us
by dying and rising to life again.
Our brother (sister) N. was faithful
and believed in our own resurrection.
Give to him (her) the joys and blessings
of the life to come.
We ask this through our Lord Jesus Christ,
    your Son,
who lives and reigns with you and the Holy Spirit,
one God, for ever and ever.

— *MASSES FOR THE DEAD (SECOND ANNIVERSARY MASS)*

For a Departed Child

May we become as this little child who now follows the Child Jesus, that Lamb of God, in a white robe whithersoever He goes; even so, Lord Jesus, Thou gavest him (her) to us, Thou hast taken him (her) from us. Blessed be the Name of the Lord. Blessed be our God for ever and ever. Amen.

— *JOHN EVELYN, 1620*

A Biography of the Author

Glenn M. Spencer, Jr., studied philosophy at
Elon College in North Carolina and English
literature at the University of North Carolina
at Greensboro and holds a master of divinity
degree from the Divinity School at Duke
University. He has served as chaplain at
Duke University Medical Center and
Director of Pastoral Care at Charter Medical
Center of Greensboro, North Carolina. He is
a priest in the Anglican Church in America
and Rector of All Saints Anglican Church in
Charlottesville, Virginia. He teaches
dogmatic theology and pastoral care for his
diocesan training academy, St. Augustine's,
and he presents workshops for other
professional caregivers in the field of grief
and loss.

Our Sunday Visitor...
Your Source for Discovering the Riches of the Catholic Faith

Our Sunday Visitor has an extensive line of materials for young children, teens, and adults. Our books, Bibles, booklets, CD-ROMs, audios, and videos are available in bookstores worldwide.

To receive a FREE full-line catalog or for more information, call **Our Sunday Visitor** at **1-800-348-2440**. Or write, **Our Sunday Visitor** / 200 Noll Plaza / Huntington, IN 46750.

Please send me: __ A catalog
Please send me materials on:
  __ Apologetics and catechetics   __ Reference works
  __ Prayer books   __ Heritage and the saints
  __ The family   __ The parish

Name_____
Address_____Apt._____
City_____State___Zip_____
Telephone (   )_____
                                    A93BBABP

Please send a friend: __ A catalog
Please send a friend materials on:
  __ Apologetics and catechetics   __ Reference works
  __ Prayer books   __ Heritage and the saints
  __ The family   __ The parish

Name_____
Address_____Apt._____
City_____State___Zip_____
Telephone (   )_____
                                    A93BBABP

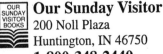

Our Sunday Visitor
200 Noll Plaza
Huntington, IN 46750
1-800-348-2440
osvbooks@osv.com

Your Source for Discovering the Riches of the Catholic Faith